THE HIKERS GUIDE TO O'AHU

THE HIKERS GUIDE TO O'AHU

Stuart M. Ball, Jr.

A KOLOWALU BOOK
UNIVERSITY OF HAWAII PRESS
HONOLULU

Library of Congress Cataloging-in-Publication Data
Ball, Stuart M., 1948–
    The hikers guide to O'ahu / Stuart M. Ball, Jr.
        p.   cm.
    Includes bibliographical references (p.) and index.
    ISBN 0-8248-1513-0
    1. Hiking—Hawaii—Oahu—Guidebooks.   2. Oahu (Hawaii)–
    –Guidebooks.   I. Title.
    GV199.42.H32O143   1993
    919.69'3—dc20   93-5507
                                                       CIP

University of Hawaii Press books are printed on acid-free
paper and meet the guidelines for permanence and durability
of the Council on Library Resources

Maps by Manoa Mapworks, Inc.

Designed by Paula Newcomb

CONTENTS

Color illustrations follow p. 138

INTRODUCTION

Nobody hikes on Oʻahu! I'm exaggerating, of course, but on a typical weekend the beaches are jammed, and the mountains are virtually empty. This book aims to change that just a little. It will take you to lush valleys, spectacular waterfalls, and windswept ridges, where few people go.

This guide includes most of the day hikes on Oʻahu, 79 to be exact. Fifty-three of them are open to the public and are described in detail. The remaining 26 are closed hikes and thus rate only a brief description in the Appendix.

This book does not include the tourist walks, such as Diamond Head. Also not included are hikes that no one has done for decades, such as Kahuku. The magnificent Koʻolau Summit Trail is also left out because it does not lend itself to day hiking.

This guide is primarily a book of routes. It does not describe Oʻahu's fascinating plants, birds, and rocks in detail. (It will, however, tell you how to get to places where you can see them.) The best way to learn about them is to go hiking with a club.

There are two hiking clubs on Oʻahu. The Hawaiian Trail and Mountain Club offers hikes most Sundays and some Saturdays. For their current schedule send a self-addressed, stamped envelope to P.O. Box 2238, Honolulu, HI 96804. The Sierra Club, Hawaiʻi Chapter, also hikes on Sundays. For more information, call them at 538-6616 or write them at P.O. Box 2577, Honolulu, HI 96803. Both clubs list their hikes in the current events section of the daily newspapers.

The two clubs have very different styles. HTM is a pure hiking club that offers an extensive schedule with a good variety of hikes. You go at your own pace on their outings. The Sierra Club is primarily involved with conservation issues and projects. They offer a limited schedule of mostly easy hikes. Their leaders usually keep the group together and explain the natural history of the area. Take your pick.

Let me end with a note of caution. On the day it was printed this guidebook became out of date because conditions change. A landowner revises his access policy. New housing construction forces a trailhead to be moved. A winter storm causes a landslide that blocks the trail. Do not rely entirely on this book; use your own judgment and common sense, as well.

Good luck and good hiking!

HIKING TIPS

What to Wear

For short, easy hikes, wear:
    hiking boots, running or walking shoes (must have a tread)
    tabis (Japanese reef walkers, for gulch hikes only)
    socks
    light cotton pants (no jeans) or shorts (if you don't mind getting scratched)
    light cotton shirt (quick drying)
    rain jacket

For long, tough hikes, add:
    light wool sweater or polypropylene shirt
    work gloves

What to Bring

For short, easy hikes, bring:
    daypack
    1 quart water
    lunch
    sunscreen

For long, tough hikes, add:
    extra water
    extra food
    first aid kit
    space blanket
    flashlight and extra bulb and batteries
    compass
    topographic map

Pack It Out

Do not leave any trash on the trail. Pack it out! Trash includes cigarette butts, gum wrappers, orange peels, and apple cores.

Clidemia hirta

Clidemia is an aggressive weed that overgrows many of the trails in the wet sections of the Koʻolau and Waiʻanae Ranges. The shrub is easily recognizable by its bright green, elliptical leaves, which are heavily creased. Mature plants have hairy blue berries containing lots of tiny seeds.

Clidemia is spread by birds and, yes, hikers. Clean the soles and sides of your boots carefully after hiking in infested areas.

Hazards

Hiking in Oʻahu's mountains is probably safer than walking around Honolulu. Nevertheless, there are hazards in hiking, as in any sport. Specific hazards, such as a rough, overgrown trail or a steep, narrow spot, are detailed in the individual hike descriptions. Described below are some of the general hazards that you should be aware of.

Too Hot:

Hiking on Oʻahu is usually a hot, sweaty experience. You can become dehydrated very easily. Lack of water may lead to heat exhaustion and heat stroke.

The need for water on a hike varies from person to person. You will soon learn how much you need to bring. As a general rule, take 1 quart of water on the short, easy hikes. Take 2 or more quarts on the long, tough hikes.

Drink plenty of water throughout the hike. If you have to ration or borrow water, you didn't bring enough.

Too Cold:

Hiking on Oʻahu can sometimes be a wet, cold experience. In winter, a Kona storm with high winds and heavy rainfall can make you very cold very quickly. Insufficient or inappropriate clothing leads to chilling, which leads to hypothermia.

Always bring a rain jacket for protection from wind and rain. Most of the time you won't even take it out of your pack, but bring it anyway! Also, on the long ridge hikes take a light wool sweater or polypropylene shirt, which will keep you warm even when wet.

Leptospirosis:

Leptospirosis is a bacterial disease found in freshwater ponds and streams contaminated with the urine of rats, mice, and mongooses. The bacteria can enter the body through the nose, mouth, eyes, or open cuts.

Symptoms resemble those of the flu—fever, chills, sweating, head and muscle aches, weakness, diarrhea, and vomiting. They may persist for a few days to several weeks. In rare cases the symptoms may become more severe and even lead to death.

What to do? First, never drink any stream water unless you have adequately boiled, filtered, or chemically treated it. That's easy. None of the hikes in this book is so long that you cannot bring all the water you need with you. Second, on the stream hikes wear pants to avoid getting cut and don't go swimming. That's harder for some people to do. You have to decide how much risk you are willing to take. If you played it conservatively and never crossed a stream or swam in a pool, you would eliminate ⅓ of the hikes in this book!

Goat/Pig Hunters:

On some of the hikes you will meet goat or pig hunters. They are friendly people, and their dogs usually are, too. They use hiking trails to access hunting areas. However, the hunt usually takes place off trail.

Stay away from areas where you hear shots being fired or dogs barking.

Marijuana (pakalōlō) Growers:

The danger from marijuana growers and their booby traps is grossly exaggerated. The growers do not plant their plots near recognized trails. All the hikes in this book travel on established trails. Stay on the trail, and you should have no pakalōlō problems.

Hiking Alone

Hiking alone is generally not recommended, but who can resist doing it occasionally? You go at your own pace. You see more of everything. If you do hike alone, remember to tell someone where you are going and when you will be out. Make sure they know to call the emergency number (911) and ask for Fire Rescue if you don't call or show up on time.

Getting Lost

Don't do it! Seriously, take along this book and follow the hike narrative closely. Memorize key junctions. Constantly be aware of the route you are traveling. Remember, you may not know where you are, but if you know where you came from, you're not lost.

The mountains are a dangerous place for disoriented, tired, hungry hikers. If you do become completely lost, settle down for the night and wait for rescue. You did let someone know where you were hiking, right? You did bring your sweater and space blanket, right?

A Final Caution

Descriptions of the accessibility and degree of difficulty of the hikes described in this book should be taken as general guidelines only. Your level of physical fitness and hiking experience may qualify the description of a particular hike as "novice," "intermediate," or "expert." Similarly, a danger rating of "low" or "medium" should not be taken as a guarantee that the hike is safe. YOU HAVE TO DECIDE HOW MUCH RISK YOU ARE WILLING TO TAKE.

HIKE CATEGORIES

Type

There are three types of hikes on O'ahu: ridge, valley, and foothill. Ridge hikes climb a ridge to the summit of a mountain or a mountain range. Valley hikes follow a valley bottom upstream. In both types the route out is usually the same as the route in.

Foothill hikes cut across the topography. They cross a ridge, descend into a valley, and so on. They do this at lower elevations where the topography is relatively gentle. Foothill hikes are usually loop hikes.

There are two types of trails on ridge hikes: graded and ungraded. An ungraded trail sticks to the crest of the ridge with all of its ups and downs. A graded trail is built into the side of the ridge just below its top. Although avoiding drastic elevation changes, a graded trail works into and out of every ravine along the flank of the ridge.

Length

Length is the distance covered on the entire hike. If the hike is point to point, the length is one way. If the hike is out and back, the length is round trip. If the hike is a loop, the length is the complete loop.

Length is measured on the U.S. Geological Survey topographic maps. The plotted distance is then increased by 10 to 20 percent and rounded to the nearest mile. The percentage increase attempts to account for trail meandering too small to be shown on the map.

None of the trails on O'ahu has been measured precisely.

Elevation Gain

Elevation gain is measured from the lowest to the highest point on the hike and then rounded to the nearest 100 ft. No attempt is made to account for the ups and downs in between. The measurements are taken from the U.S. Geological Survey topographic maps.

Danger

Danger indicates the extent of sections where a narrow trail and a steep slope combine to produce a severe hazard. A fall in one of those areas could result in serious injury or death.

The categories are low, medium, and high. A rating of low or medium does not imply that the hike is safe.

Suitable for

Use the suitability index to find out which hikes best match your hiking ability. The categories are novice, intermediate, and expert. Novices are beginning hikers. Experts are experienced hikers. Intermediates are those in between.

Hikes for novices only are short with little elevation gain. The trail is wide and clear. Hikes for experts only involve considerable climbing, often on a narrow, rough, overgrown trail. Those are the extremes. As you will see, most hikes fall in between. Some are even suitable for everyone because they start out easy and then get progressively harder the farther you go.

Remember, how difficult a hike seems to you depends on your hiking experience and physical fitness. An experienced conditioned hiker will find the novice hikes easy and the expert hikes difficult. An out-of-shape beginner may well find some of the novice hikes challenging.

Use the suitability index only as a rough guide. Read the description to get a better feel for the hike.

Location

Location tells the general area of the hike. Given is the nearest town or subdivision. Also mentioned is the mountain range (Koʻolau or Waiʻanae) and the side of the range (leeward or windward) where the hike is to be found.

Topo Map

Topo map refers to the U.S. Geological Survey quadrangle that shows the area of the hike. All maps referenced are in the 7.5 minute topographic series with a scale of 1:24,000 and a contour interval of 40 ft.

In Honolulu, topographic maps are available from Pacific Map Center at 250 Ward Avenue, Suite 220 (phone 591–1200).

Access

There are two categories of access: open and conditional.

You may do OPEN hikes anytime without restriction.

You may do CONDITIONAL hikes subject to the terms required by the landowner. They usually include obtaining verbal or written permission. You may have to sign a liability waiver. In addition, there may be restrictions on the size and composition of the group and the time when you can do the hike.

The specific conditions are described in the individual descriptions of the hikes in this category. If you do not adhere to those conditions, you are trespassing.

The two clubs mentioned in the introduction offer a good means of doing conditional hikes. The club gets the required permissions, saving you time and trouble. Check their schedules.

In addition to the hikes described in detail in this book, there are numerous hikes that are currently closed to the general public. See the Appendix for a list and brief description of them.

Trailhead Directions

Trailhead directions are detailed driving instructions from downtown Honolulu to the start of the hike. If you are familiar with O'ahu, these directions should be sufficient to get you to the trailhead. If you are unfamiliar with the island, bring along a copy of Bryan's O'ahu Sectional Maps or James A. Bier's O'ahu Reference Maps to supplement the directions. Both show the start of many of the hikes. Both maps can be purchased locally at book stores.

For some hikes the directions stop short of the actual trailhead. There are two reasons for suggesting that you do some extra road walking. First, it is generally safer to park your car on a main road, rather than on a back road.

Second, the dirt roads leading to some of the trailheads are narrow, rough, and often muddy. The directions assume that you have a two-wheel-drive car and that the road is dry. With a four-wheel-drive vehicle you may be able to get closer to the trailhead. On the other hand, if the road is muddy, you may not even be able to drive as far as the directions recommend.

Route Description

This section provides a detailed description of the route that the hike follows. Out and back hikes are described on the way in. Loop hikes and point-to-point hikes are described in the preferred direction.

Each hike has its own map. The solid line shows the route. The letters indicate important junctions, landmarks, and interesting points. They are keyed to a description in the narrative. For example, map point A is always where you park your car.

The maps are reproductions of the U.S. Geological Survey quadrangles for the immediate area of the hike. As in the originals, the scale is 1:24,000 and the contour interval is 40 ft.

Many of the trails are marked by surveyor's ribbon of various colors. Do not, however, follow those markers blindly. They may not take you where you want to go!

Some of the trailheads have new brown-and-yellow signs. They have been put up by the Forestry and Wildlife Division of the State Department of Land and Natural Resources under their Na Ala Hele Trail and Access System Program. It involves trail marking, maintenance, and access. Some of the closed hikes may open up in the future because of their efforts.

The word *contour* is sometimes used in the route description as a verb, that is, to contour. It means to hike at roughly the same elevation across a slope. Contouring generally occurs on trails that are cut into the flank of a ridge and work into and out of each side gulch.

Notes

The notes section provides additional information about the hike to make it safer and more enjoyable. There are notes about trail conditions, obscure junctions, hazardous sections, flash flooding, and side trails to explore. Other notes mention good views, ripe fruit, deep swimming holes, interesting plants, hungry mosquitoes, and the best time of year to do the hike.

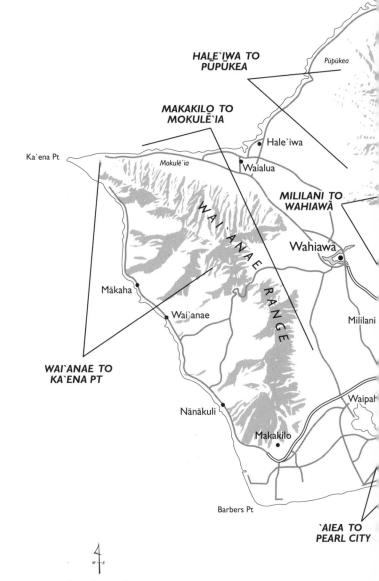

HALE`IWA TO
PŪPŪKEA

Pūpūkea

MAKAKILO TO
MOKULĒ`IA

Hale`iwa

Ka`ena Pt

Mokulē`ia

Waialua

MILILANI TO
WAHIAWĀ

Wahiawā

Mākaha

Wai`anae

Mililani

WAI`ANAE TO
KA`ENA PT

Waipah

Nānākuli

Makakilo

Barbers Pt

`AIEA TO
PEARL CITY

Kahuku P

N
W—E

Manoa Mapworks, Inc.

Māma

KAHANA
TO LĀ`IE

O`AHU

huku

Lā`ie

Hau`ula

KO`OLAU RANGE

Kahana

Ka`a`awa

WAIMĀNALO
TO KA`A`AWA

Kāne`ohe

Bay

Kailua
Bay

Pearl City

Hālawa

`Aiea

Kāne`ohe

Kailua

Pearl
Harbor

Kālihi

Waimānalo
Bay

Waimānalo

Nu`uanu

Mānoa

Hawai`i Kai

Makapu`u Pt

HONOLULU

`Aina Haina

LIHI TO
ĀLAWA

Kaimuki

Maunalua Bay

Waikīkī

MĀNOA TO
NU`UANU

a y

HAWAI`I KAI TO KAIMUKĪ

Hike Summary

Hike	Location	Type*	Length (mi)	Elev. Gain (ft)	Access	Novice	Int.	Expert	Narrow Spots	Views	Swimming	Native Plants/Birds
Leeward Koʻolau Range												
1. Koko Crater	Hawaiʻi Kai	R	3	1,000	Open		X		X	X		
2. Kuliʻouʻou Ridge	Kuliʻouʻou	R	5	2,000	Open		X	X	X	X		
3. Kuliʻouʻou Valley	Kuliʻouʻou	V	2	300	Open	X						X
4. Lanipō	Maunalani Heights	R	7	1,700	Open		X			X		X
5. Hawaiʻiloa Ridge	Hawaiʻi Loa	R	5	1,400	Cond.	X	X			X		X
6. Waʻahila-Kolowalu	St. Louis Heights	R	3	1,100	Open	X	X			X		
7. ʻAihualama-ʻŌhiʻa	Mānoa	F	8	1,700	Open	X	X			X		
8. Makiki-Tantalus	Makiki	F	8	1,500	Open	X	X			X	X	
9. Nuʻuanu	Nuʻuanu	F	5	1,000	Open	X	X			X	X	
10. Kamanaiki	Kalihi	R	5	1,300	Open	X	X			X		
11. Bowman	Fort Shafter	R	12	2,400	Open		X	X		X		X
12. Tripler Ridge	Tripler	R	11	2,100	Cond.	X	X	X	X	X		X
13. Puʻu Keahi a Kahoe	Moanalua	R	11	2,600	Cond.		X	X	X	X		X
14. Moanalua Valley	Moanalua	V	11	1,400	Cond.	X	X			X	X	
15. ʻAiea Loop	ʻAiea	F	5	900	Open	X				X		
16. ʻAiea Ridge	ʻAiea	R	11	1,700	Open	X	X	X		X		X
17. Kalauao	ʻAiea	V	4	700	Open	X				X		
18. Waimano Ridge	Pearl City	R	15	1,700	Open		X	X		X	X	X
19. Waimano Valley	Pearl City	V	2	300	Open	X						
20. Waimano Pool	Pacific Palisades	V	3	600	Open	X	X				X	
21. Mānana	Pacific Palisades	R	12	1,700	Open	X	X	X		X		X
22. Waikakalaua	Mililani	V	3	200	Cond.	X						
23. Schofield-Waikāne	Wahiawā	R	12	1,000	Cond.	X	X	X		X	X	X
24. Wahiawā Hills	Wahiawā	F	5	600	Cond.		X				X	
25. Poamoho Ridge	Helemano	R	12	1,000	Cond.	X	X	X		X	X	X
26. ʻŌpaeʻula	Haleʻiwa	V	2	200	Cond.	X					X	X

Site	Location	Type	Size	Elev. (ft)	Status							
27. Kawai Iki	Hale'iwa	V	5	200	Cond.	X				X	X	X
28. Kawainui	Hale'iwa	V	6	600	Cond.	X				X	X	X
29. Kawailoa Ridge	Hale'iwa	R	11	1,100	Cond.				X	X	X	
30. Kaunala	Pūpūkea	F	6	400	Cond.	X			X	X	X	
Windward Ko'olau Range												
31. Olomana	Maunawili	R	5	1,600	Cond.				X	X	X	
32. Ko'olaupoko	Maunawili	F	5	600	Open	X				X	X	X
33. Old Pali Road	Nu'uanu Pali	F	3	500	Open	X		X		X	X	
34. Likeke	Kāne'ohe	F	5	100	Open			X				
35. Pu'u Manamana	Kahana	R	4	2,100	Open				X	X	X	
36. Kahana Valley	Kahana	V	8	400	Open	X				X	X	X
37. Pu'u Piei	Kahana	R	2	1,700	Open	X			X	X	X	
38. Sacred Falls	Hau'ula	V	5	300	Open	X				X		X
39. Hau'ula-Papali	Hau'ula	F	6	1,500	Open	X				X	X	
40. Ma'akua Gulch	Hau'ula	V	6	900	Open					X	X	X
41. Koloa Gulch	Lā'ie	V	8	1,200	Cond.	X				X	X	X
42. Lā'ie	Lā'ie	R	12	2,200	Cond.				X	X	X	X
Windward Wai'anae Range												
43. Pālehua	Makakilo	F	9	1,500	Cond.	X			X	X	X	X
44. Palikea	Village Park	R	8	2,300	Cond.				X	X	X	X
45. Pu'u Kaua	Kunia	R	5	2,000	Cond.			X	X	X	X	X
46. Kānehoa-Hāpapa	Kunia	R	5	1,900	Cond.	X		X	X	X	X	X
47. Pu'u Kalena	Schofield Barracks	R	5	1,900	Cond.			X	X	X	X	X
48. Dupont	Waialua	R	11	4,000	Cond.			X	X	X	X	
49. Keālia	Mokulē'ia	R	7	1,900	Open			X	X	X	X	
Leeward Wai'anae Range												
50. Wai'anae Ka'ala	Wai'anae	R	5	2,600	Open	X			X	X	X	X
51. 'Ōhikilolo	Mākua	R	7	3,000	Cond.	X			X	X	X	X
52. Wai'anae Kai	Wai'anae	F	3	1,300	Open	X				X	X	
53. Kuaokalā	Ka'ena	F	6	800	Cond.	X				X	X	X

* F, foothill; R, ridge; V, valley.

Leeward Ko'olau Range

HAWAI'I KAI TO KAIMUKĪ

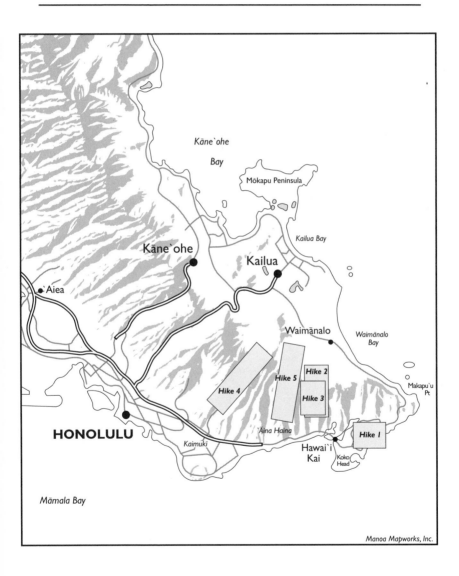

Kāne'ohe Bay

Mōkapu Peninsula

Kailua Bay

Kāne'ohe

Kailua

'Aiea

Waimānalo

Waimānalo Bay

Hike 2

Hike 5

Hike 4

Hike 3

Makapu'u Pt

'Āina Haina

HONOLULU

Kaimukī

Hawai'i Kai

Koko Head

Hike 1

Māmala Bay

Manoa Mapworks, Inc.

1 Koko Crater

Type:	Ungraded ridge
Length:	3 mi round trip
Elev. Gain:	1,000 ft
Danger:	Medium
Suitable for:	Intermediate
Location:	Leeward Koʻolau Range above Hawaiʻi Kai
Topo Map:	Koko Head
Access:	Open

Trailhead Directions

At Ward Ave. get on the Lunalilo Fwy (H-1) Koko Head bound (east).

As the freeway ends, continue straight on Kalanianaʻole Hwy (Rte 72).

Pass ʻĀina Haina and Niu Valley Center and enter Hawaiʻi Kai.

Just past Koko Marina Shopping Center, turn left on Lunalilo Home Rd.

At the fourth traffic light, by Kamiloiki Community Park, turn right on Hawaiʻi Kai Dr.

At the end of the road, turn right on Kealahou St. by the Hawaiʻi Kai Golf Course.

Take the first right, marked Koko Crater Stables.

The road becomes dirt and turns sharp left.

Park on the right by the entrance to the stables (map point A).

Route Description

Walk around the chain and enter Koko Crater Botanic Garden.

Follow the dirt road through a plumeria grove.

Another dirt road comes in on the right.

At the end of the grove, reach a junction with the dirt road that loops inside the crater (map point B). Turn left on to the loop road.

Pass a paddock on the left.

The road splits. Take the right fork into the crater.

The road narrows and ascends gradually through a forest of haole koa and kiawe.

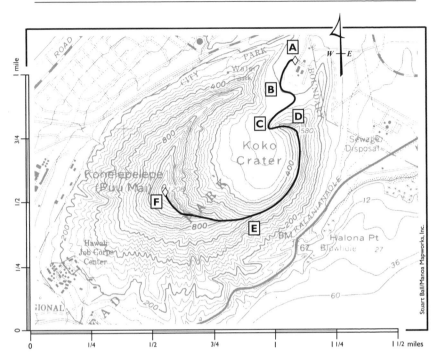

Reach another fork by a large white-barked tree (map point C). Bear left and up on a bridle path.

Almost immediately bear left again on a trail heading up the ridge.

Climb steeply, at times on bare rock.

Keep right, following the side ridge up.

Reach the crater rim and turn right along it (map point D).

Bear right off the ridge line to avoid a rock face.

Cross a relatively level section as the ridge alternately widens and narrows.

Begin climbing, gradually at first, and then more steeply.

About 25 yd below a small triangular peak, reach a junction (map point E). Continue along the rim. (The trail to the left leads down to the Hālona Blowhole parking lot and is an alternate route for this hike.)

Traverse a narrow, rocky section. Stay on top of the ridge.

Bear right around a large balanced rock.

Negotiate another narrow stretch.

Keep left to bypass a rock face.

Cross some barbed wire on the ground.

Pass two small concrete structures on the right and some utility poles on the left.

Reach Pu'u Ma'i (elev. 1,208 ft), the highest point on the crater rim (map point F). At the top is a metal platform and the remains of an inclined railway.

Notes

Koko Crater is a windy hike. The tradewinds hit the island head on here so be prepared to get blown around. The wind keeps the vegetation low, so the trail rarely becomes overgrown. The path is rough and narrow in some spots, though. Watch your footing constantly.

From the top are good views of Sandy Beach, Koko Head, Hanauma Bay, and the Ko'olau Range. You can see the leeward coast to Diamond Head and the skyscrapers of Waikiki. On a clear day the islands of Moloka'i, Lāna'i, and Maui are visible to the east.

On the way down remember to keep left where the rim splits into two spur ridges.

It is possible to continue along the rim to make a complete loop; however, the 'ewa (west) side is crumbly and very narrow. Gusts of wind make that stretch even more challenging.

The loop road inside the crater through the botanic garden makes a short novice hike.

An alternate route to Koko Crater starts from the Hālona Blowhole parking lot. Walk along the road toward Hanauma Bay. At the end of the guard rail on the right take the spur ridge up the side of the crater. Part way up, the trail crosses a small rock bridge. This route is shorter, but steeper, than the approach from the stables.

2 Kuli'ou'ou Ridge

Type:	Ungraded ridge
Length:	5 mi round trip
Elev. Gain:	2,000 ft
Danger:	High
Suitable for:	Novice, Intermediate, Expert
Location:	Leeward Ko'olau Range above Kuli'ou'ou
Topo Map:	Koko Head
Access:	Open

Trailhead Directions

At Ward Ave. get on the Lunalilo Fwy (H-1) Koko Head bound (east).

As the freeway ends, continue straight on Kalaniana'ole Hwy (Rte 72).

Drive by 'Āina Haina and Niu Valley Center.

Pass Holy Trinity Catholic Church on the right.

Turn left on 'Elelupe Rd. by the Kuli'ou'ou Booster Pumping Station and head into Kuli'ou'ou Valley.

Just after making a sharp right, turn left on Kuli'ou'ou Rd.

Pass Kuli'ou'ou Neighborhood Park on the right.

At the dead end sign turn right on Kala'au Pl.

Park on the street just before it ends at a turnaround circle (map point A).

Route Description

At the back of the circle take the one-lane, paved road on the left leading down to Kuli'ou'ou Stream.

Before crossing the stream, bear right on a grassy road.

Enter a clearing with a lone Christmas berry tree in the middle.

The road narrows and becomes the Kuli'ou'ou Valley Trail.

Begin contouring above the stream through a mixed, exotic forest.

Cross a small gully.

Reach a junction (map point B). Turn sharp right and up on the Kuli'ou'ou Ridge Trail. It is narrow, but graded. (The Kuli'ou'ou Valley Trail continues straight, into the valley.)

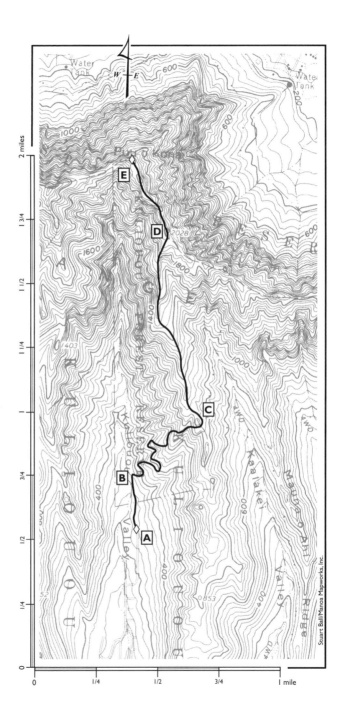

Climb gradually up the side of the valley on 10 long switchbacks. Between the second and third one a trail comes in on the left. Keep right and up.

Ascend a side ridge briefly.

Continue climbing via two short switchbacks.

Just before the top, make your way up a gully lined with ironwood trees.

Reach the ridge line in a grove of ironwoods and Norfolk Island pines (map point C). Turn left up the ridge.

Pass a makeshift lean-to on the left.

Wind through a stand of large Norfolk Island pines.

Cross an eroded spot.

Pass two covered picnic tables on the right.

In a grove of ironwoods pass a large, flat area used as a camp site.

As the ridge broadens, keep to its left side.

Enter a forest of tall Norfolk Island pines and ironwoods.

Climb, steeply at times, through a dying 'ōhi'a grove.

Reach the Ko'olau summit at an eroded hill (elev. 2,028 ft) (map point D).

Turn left along the summit ridge.

Bypass a rock face to the left and then descend the next one.

Go around a third rock face to the left.

Climb through two eroded spots with loose rock.

Reach Pu'u o Kona (elev. 2,200 ft), a flat-topped mountain that juts out on the windward side (map point E).

Notes

Kuli'ou'ou Ridge is one of the finest hikes on the island. It offers something for everyone. The stretch along the Ko'olau summit to Pu'u o Kona is a real challenge for experienced hikers. Intermediate hikers can climb to the eroded hill on the summit. Novices can hike as far as they want.

I'm not kidding, though, when I rated the entire hike for experts. It is one of only a handful of hikes in this book that go along the Ko'olau summit. The rock there is loose and crumbly. There are several narrow, tricky spots.

The views on this hike are world class. You can see the leeward coast from Koko Head to Honolulu, the Ko'olau range from Makapu'u Point to Kōnāhuanui, and the windward coast from Waimānalo to Kualoa Point.

Memorize the junction of the switchback and ridge trails for the return trip.

The trail receives periodic maintenance. The upper section is overgrown between clearings. The rest of the hike is usually clear.

The initial section by the stream is also part of the Kuli'ou'ou Valley hike.

3 Kuli'ou'ou Valley

Type:	Valley
Length:	2 mi round trip
Elev. Gain:	300 ft
Danger:	Low
Suitable for:	Novice
Location:	Leeward Ko'olau Range above Kuli'ou'ou
Topo Map:	Koko Head
Access:	Open

Trailhead Directions

At Ward Ave. get on the Lunalilo Fwy (H-1) Koko Head bound (east).
As the freeway ends, continue straight on Kalaniana'ole Hwy (Rte 72).
Drive by 'Āina Haina and Niu Valley Center.
Pass Holy Trinity Catholic Church on the right.
Turn left on 'Elelupe Rd. by the Kuli'ou'ou Booster Pumping Station and head into Kuli'ou'ou Valley.
Just after making a sharp right, turn left on Kuli'ou'ou Rd.
Pass Kuli'ou'ou Neighborhood Park on the right.
At the dead end sign turn right on Kala'au Pl.
Park on the street just before it ends at a turnaround circle (map point A).

Route Description

At the back of the circle take the one-lane, paved road on the left leading down to Kuli'ou'ou Stream.
Before crossing the stream, bear right on a grassy road.
Enter a clearing with a lone Christmas berry tree in the middle.
The road narrows and becomes the Kuli'ou'ou Valley Trail.
Begin contouring above the stream through a mixed, exotic forest.
Cross a small gully.
Reach a junction (map point B). Continue straight on the Kuli'ou'ou Valley Trail. (The trail on the right switchbacks up the side of the valley and is the Kuli'ou'ou Ridge Trail.)

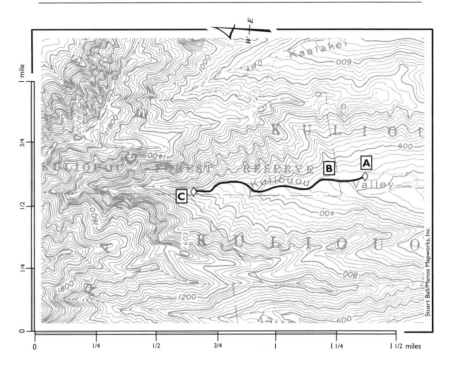

Cross several more small gullies and then two larger ones. The last one has a small waterfall chute.

Shortly afterward, reach the end of the improved trail under a spreading Christmas berry tree by the stream (map point C).

Notes

Kuli'ou'ou Valley is a great hike for beginners. It's short, shady, and usually dry. The trail is well graded and receives regular maintenance.

There are some mosquitoes on this hike.

Do not attempt this hike during or right after a heavy rainstorm.

Further exploration upstream is possible; however, the trail quickly becomes rough and ill defined. Eventually, it disappears altogether as the valley walls close in. Walk in the stream bed until a waterfall blocks the way.

The Kuli'ou'ou Ridge hike starts from the same trailhead.

4 Lanipō

Type:	Ungraded ridge
Length:	7 mi round trip
Elev. Gain:	1,700 ft
Danger:	Low
Suitable for:	Intermediate
Location:	Leeward Koʻolau Range above Maunalani Heights
Topo Map:	Honolulu, Koko Head
Access:	Open

Trailhead Directions

At Ward Ave. get on the Lunalilo Fwy (H-1) Koko Head bound (east).

Take the Koko Head Ave. exit (26A) in Kaimukī.

At the top of the off ramp, turn left on Koko Head Ave.

Cross Waiʻalae Ave.

At the first stop sign turn left, still on Koko Head Ave.

At the next stop sign turn right on Sierra Dr.

Switchback up the ridge to Maunalani Heights.

Pass Maunalani Playground on the right and Maunalani Nursing Center on the left.

At the end of Sierra Dr. by the last bus stop, bear right and up on Maunalani Circle.

The road swings left in a broad arc.

On the right look for a chain-link fence enclosing a Board of Water Supply tank.

Park on the street next to the fence (map point A).

Route Description

Walk back down the road to the corner of the fence.

Turn left up a narrow passageway formed by two chain-link fences. The corridor is directly across from the garage of 4970 Maunalani Circle.

At the end of the fences turn left through a small grove of ironwood trees.

Reach the crest of Mauʻumae Ridge and bear right along it.

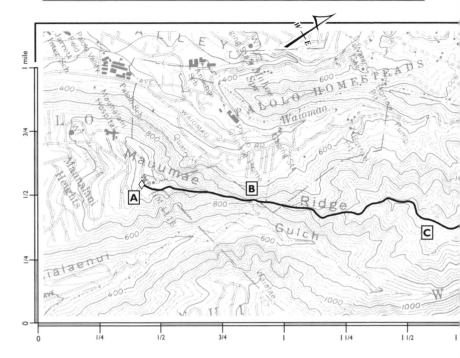

Descend moderately along the grassy, mostly open ridge with one rocky section.

Pass a utility pole on the left (map point B).

Begin a long climb interspersed with two dips.

After the second dip ascend steeply through koa. At this point the ridge is quite massive and well forested.

After a level section climb steeply again on a badly eroded trail.

Pass a large stand of ironwood trees down and on the right.

Ascend a flat grassy knob with a 360-degree view (map point C).

Enter the native rain forest dominated by 'ōhi'a and koa trees and uluhe ferns.

Climb a second knob topped by two Norfolk Island pines (map point D).

Traverse a long, relatively level section with many small ups and downs.

As the trail resumes serious climbing, look left across Pālolo Valley for Ka'au Crater and the waterfall cascading from its lip.

Go left around the edge of a short, but steep eroded spot.

The ridge narrows, and the vegetation thins.

After a stiff climb reach a flat open knob with a panoramic view (map point E).

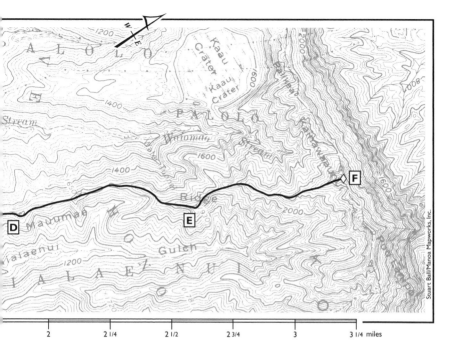

2   2 1/4   2 1/2   2 3/4   3   3 1/4 miles

Ascend steeply to a broad hump with a good view of the last stretch of the trail.

Descend the back side of the hump and go left around a slippery exposed spot.

Begin the final climb to the summit along the open windswept ridge.

As the top nears, the trail steepens and becomes severely eroded.

Reach the Koʻolau summit at a peak called Kainawaʻaunui (elev. 2,520 ft) (map point F).

Notes

Lanipō is the most popular hike to the Koʻolau summit because of its good access and relatively short length. Popular, however, does not mean crowded, even on a Sunday.

Many people are put off by the hot lower section and especially the initial rocky descent, which, of course, must be climbed on the return trip. Don't be discouraged! The native plants and the spectacular views farther in are well worth the extra effort.

From the top you can see Waimānalo Bay and much of the windward coast. Olomana with its three peaks is in front. Lanipō is the flat-topped mountain to the right along the summit ridge. The steep flanks of the Koʻolau Range from Kōnāhuanui to Puʻu o Kona are awesome. To leeward are Diamond Head and Honolulu.

Turn right along the Koʻolau summit to reach the actual peak of Lanipō. That summit section is for experienced hikers only because it is narrow, steep, and windswept.

The trail receives periodic maintenance. The middle section overgrows between clearings. The lower section is hot and dry; the upper section, cool and windy.

This hike is also known as Mauʻumae Ridge.

5 Hawai'iloa Ridge

Type:	Ungraded ridge
Length:	5 mi round trip
Elev. Gain:	1,400 ft
Danger:	Low
Suitable for:	Novice, Intermediate
Location:	Leeward Koʻolau Range above Hawaiʻi Loa
Topo Map:	Koko Head
Access:	Conditional; show an ID and sign a liability waiver at the security station on Puʻu ʻIkena Dr.

Trailhead Directions

At Ward Ave. get on the Lunalilo Fwy (H-1) Koko Head bound (east).

As the freeway ends, continue straight on Kalanianaʻole Hwy (Rte 72).

Pass ʻĀina Haina Public Library on the left.

Cross a bridge over Wailupe Stream.

At the next traffic light, by Kawaikuʻi Beach Park, turn left on Puʻu ʻIkena Dr. To make the left turn, bear right initially and then cross Kalanianaʻole Hwy.

Stop at the security station and check in.

Ascend steadily through the Hawaiʻi Loa Ridge subdivision.

At the top of the subdivision, Puʻu ʻIkena Dr. narrows and is lined with ironwood trees.

The road ends at a water tank marked Hawaiʻi Loa 1125 Reservoir.

Park in the lot on the right by the water tank (map point A).

Route Description

From the lot, walk mauka (north), crossing a gravel jogging path.

Pick up a dirt road along the crest of Hawaiʻiloa Ridge.

After crossing a rocky, eroded section, the dirt road ends (map point B).

Continue on an ungraded trail as the ridge narrows briefly.

Go through two stands of ironwoods.

Descend briefly, but steeply.

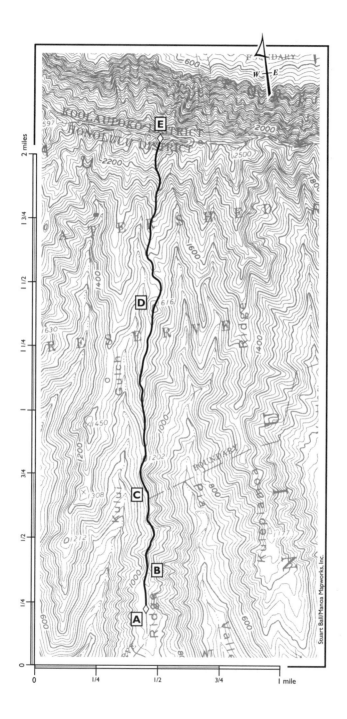

Pass a third stand of ironwoods on the left.

Traverse a relatively level section through scrub guava. In that section are two obscure junctions. Keep left each time, on the main ridge. At the first junction (map point C), the trail to the right leads a short way to a metal rod and a good view.

Ascend gradually through a long stretch of guava.

The trail briefly follows three wires that are attached to trees.

Cross a relatively level section and descend gradually, still through guava.

Pass the first patch of uluhe fern on the right.

Ascend steadily through a dark guava forest.

Reach a distinct knob, whose top is moss covered (map point D). To the side is a partial view of the summit.

Shortly afterward, the guava ends, and the native rain forest begins.

Keep right and descend steeply through uluhe.

Work to the left side of the ridge just below its top.

Turn right and up to regain the ridge line.

Work left through the uluhe as the ridge flattens.

In a small clearing surrounded by guava, swing right across the broad ridge.

Bear left and up to regain the distinct crest of the ridge.

Climb steadily along the open ridge.

The angle of ascent increases markedly.

As the top nears, the ridge widens, and the vegetation thickens.

Reach the Ko'olau summit at a small knob (elev. 2,520 ft) (map point E).

Notes

Hawai'iloa Ridge is a sleeper of a hike. It is largely unknown and thus little used. I'm not sure why, because the access is good, and the hike itself is scenic and suitable for novices and intermediates. As an added bonus, you get to see the mansions in the Hawai'i Loa Ridge subdivision.

The view from the top is quite spectacular. Below is Waimānalo town and beyond is Waimānalo Bay. Olomana is the triple-peaked mountain on the left. To the right along the summit is flat-topped Pu'u o Kona, which juts out from the ridge. Going up (down) there are views of Koko Head and Koko Crater, Diamond Head, and much of Honolulu.

The trail receives little or no maintenance. The uluhe on the upper section overgrows between clearings. The lower guava section is usually open.

The guavas are the yellow variety of strawberry guava, which is delicious. They ripen in August and September.

Leeward Ko'olau Range

MĀNOA TO NU'UANU

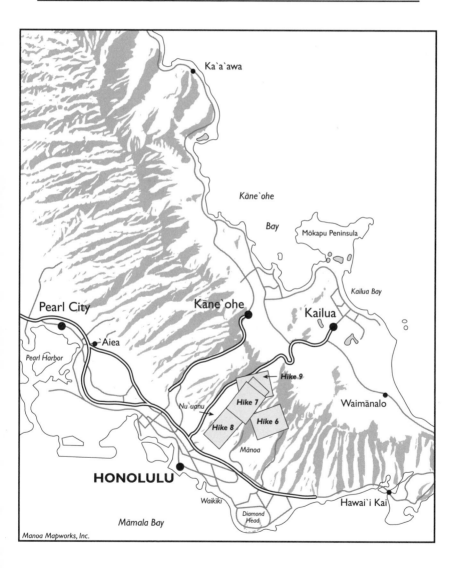

Ka`a`awa

Kāne`ohe

Bay

Mōkapu Peninsula

Kailua Bay

Pearl City

Kāne`ohe

Kailua

'Aiea

Pearl Harbor

Hike 9

Nu`uanu

Hike 7

Waimānalo

Hike 8

Hike 6

Mānoa

HONOLULU

Waikīkī

Diamond Head

Hawai`i Kai

Māmala Bay

Manoa Mapworks, Inc.

6 Waʻahila-Kolowalu

Type:	Ungraded ridge
Length:	3 mi one way
Elev. Gain:	1,100 ft (Kolowalu to Waʻahila)
Danger:	Low
Suitable for:	Novice, Intermediate
Location:	Leeward Koʻolau Range above St. Louis Heights
Topo Map:	Honolulu
Access:	Open

Trailhead Directions

To go to the Waʻahila trailhead get on the Lunalilo Fwy (H-1) at Ward Ave. Koko Head bound (east).

Take the King St. exit (25A).

Turn left underneath the freeway on to Waiʻalae Ave.

At the second traffic light, by the Chevron gas station, turn left on St. Louis Dr.

Switchback up St. Louis Heights.

A block before St. Louis Dr. ends turn right on Peter St.

Turn left on Ruth Pl. at the bus turnaround circle.

Enter Waʻahila Ridge State Recreation Area.

Park in the lot at the road end (map point A).

To go to the Kolowalu trailhead get on the Lunalilo Fwy (H-1) at Ward Ave. Koko Head bound (east).

Take the University Ave. exit (24B).

Pass the University of Hawaii on the right.

At the second traffic light after the road narrows, turn right on E. Mānoa Rd.

Pass Mānoa Marketplace on the right.

Toward the back of the valley the road splits. Take the right fork, still on E. Mānoa Rd.

At the road end turn left on Alani Dr.

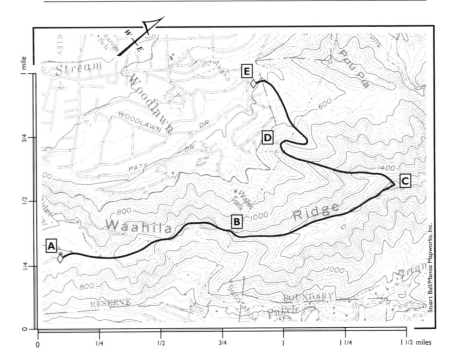

Park on Alani Dr. just before it narrows to one lane at its intersection with Woodlawn Dr. (map point E).

Route Description

At the Wa'ahila trailhead, take the paved path at the back of the parking lot.

Almost immediately cross another paved walkway and continue straight on the wide Wa'ahila Trail through the Norfolk Island pines.

Pass a small water tank on the left.

Climb steadily through a grove of strawberry guava.

Just before a level clearing turn left and down to avoid a sharp drop in Wa'ahila Ridge.

Cross a windswept section with views on both sides.

Traverse three small, but rough, humps in the ridge.

Bear right to bypass a large knob with utility poles on top (map point B).

Cross a relatively flat section of the ridge. Here the trail becomes a wide grassy avenue in spots.

A side ridge comes in on the right near a large grassy clearing.

Both the ridge and the trail become narrow and rougher.
Reach a junction (elev. 1,640 ft) (map point C). Take the wide Kolowalu Trail, which curves left and down into Mānoa Valley. (The less obvious trail to the right and up continues along Wa'ahila Ridge to Mt. Olympus on the Ko'olau summit. However, the trail is closed to the public because it goes through the Honolulu watershed.)
Descend, steeply at times, on a side ridge.
Switchback once along the side of the valley (map point D).
Bear left down a steep rocky section following a stream bed.
Cross the stream bed and work up the next side ridge.
Continue down it on a more gentle gradient.
Curve right, down to a covered picnic table.
Turn left and join a dirt road heading downhill alongside a stream.
The dirt road becomes paved Alani Dr.
Reach its intersection with Woodlawn Dr. (map point E).

Notes

Wa'ahila-Kolowalu is a good hike for beginners. It provides a short introduction to ungraded ridge walking. This hike does have some rough and steep spots, though. Take care, especially if you are new to hiking.

Most people start at the Wa'ahila trailhead and hike the ridge section out and back. For more of a workout, start at the Kolowalu trailhead and hike up to Wa'ahila Ridge. If you have two cars, do the whole hike as described. Use Dole St. to connect University Ave. with St. Louis Dr.

Along the ridge trail are good views of Mānoa Valley on the left and Pālolo Valley on the right.

The strawberry guavas usually ripen in July. Expect slim pickings, however, because of the popularity of this hike.

Wa'ahila and Kolowalu Trails receive regular maintenance and are usually open.

7 'Aihualama-'Ōhi'a (via Mānoa Falls)

Type:	Foothill
Length:	8 mi round trip
Elev. Gain:	1,700 ft
Danger:	Low
Suitable for:	Novice, Intermediate
Location:	Leeward Ko'olau Range above Mānoa
Topo Map:	Honolulu
Access:	Open

Trailhead Directions

Get on S. King St. Koko Head bound (east).

Turn left on Punahou St. by the Cinerama Theater.

Pass Punahou School on the right and enter Mānoa Valley.

The road narrows to two lanes and splits. Take the left fork on to Mānoa Rd.

At the stop sign proceed straight across the intersection on a much wider Mānoa Rd.

Pass Mānoa Elementary School on the right.

Park on Mānoa Rd. just before it narrows. That's at its intersection with Wa'akaua St. (map point A).

Route Description

Continue along Mānoa Rd. on foot.

Walk underneath the pedestrian overpass at the entrance to Paradise Park.

Follow the main road as it curves left and then right around the lower parking lot of the park.

As the paved road turns left to Lyon Arboretum, proceed straight on a dirt road (map point B).

The road narrows and becomes Mānoa Falls Trail.

Cross a small stream on a bridge.

Bear left to parallel a second, larger stream that soon splits to form

24

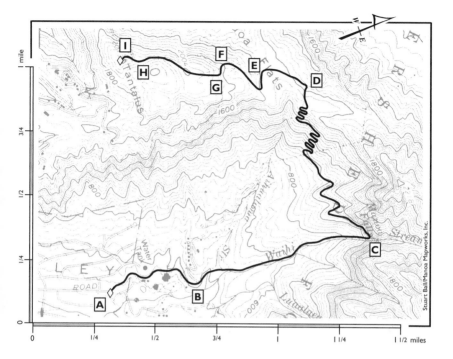

'Aihualama and Waihī streams. (Just below the split an obscure side trail crosses the main stream and leads to Lua'alaea Falls.)

Bear right and cross 'Aihualama Stream. (Just before the crossing, another side trail, on the left, heads up 'Aihualama Stream through the back of Lyon Arboretum.)

Negotiate a very rocky, rooty stretch.

Waihī Stream comes in on the right.

Ascend gradually alongside it. The trail is well defined, but badly eroded. Some sections are paved with rocks.

Climb more steeply now as the valley narrows.

Reach Mānoa Falls with its swimming hole (map point C).

Backtrack along the trail to the first group of trees.

There, turn right and up on the 'Aihualama Trail.

Work in and out of three gulches.

Break out into the open under some utility lines. (Just past the lines a faint side trail on the left leads back down to 'Aihualama Stream.)

Climb the side of Mānoa Valley on 14 switchbacks.

Enter a bamboo forest at the top of the ridge.

Reach a junction with the Pauoa Flats Trail (map point D). Turn left on it. (To the right the flats trail leads to an overlook of Nu'uanu Valley.)

Reach another junction. Continue straight on the flats trail. (To the right the Nu'uanu Trail leads down to the Judd Trail and Nu'uanu Valley.)

Right after the Nu'uanu junction the trail forks (map point E). Take the left fork, still on the flats trail. (The right fork connects with the Mānoa Cliff Trail and Tantalus Dr.)

Climb steadily up the flank of Tantalus. There is one switchback.

Reach a junction with the Mānoa Cliff Trail (map point F). Turn left on it. (To the right the cliff trail leads to Tantalus Dr.)

Begin contouring around the side of Tantalus.

Reach another junction (map point G). Turn sharp right and up on the Pu'u 'Ōhi'a Trail. (The cliff trail continues straight, to Round Top Dr.)

Ascend gradually through solid bamboo.

Reach a Hawaiian Telephone installation and go around it to the right.

Turn right on a one-lane paved road.

The road dips and then climbs gradually.

Reach an intersection (map point H). Take the road on the left heading up Tantalus. (The road on the right leads down to Tantalus Dr. The Pu'u 'Ōhi'a Trail continues on the left, descending steeply to Tantalus Dr.)

The road ends at a second Hawaiian Telephone installation with a tower.

Take the path by the utility pole.

Reach the summit of Tantalus (Pu'u 'Ōhi'a) (elev. 2,013 ft), which is marked by a concrete platform (map point I).

Notes

'Aihualama-'Ōhi'a is one of several routes to the top of Tantalus. The others are all much easier; however, with this route you know you've really climbed the mountain. Novices can go as far as Mānoa Falls.

The hike to Mānoa Falls is popular with both tourists and locals. The swimming hole can get quite crowded on a sunny weekend. Beyond the falls you should see fewer people. There are a lot of mosquitos on the falls trail.

From the top of Tantalus you can see Diamond Head and much of Honolulu. Mauka is the Ko'olau Range with the prominent summits of Kōnāhuanui in front and Mt. Olympus on the right.

The side trip to Tantalus Crater is well worthwhile. From the top retrace your steps to the road intersection. Turn right on the Pu'u 'Ōhi'a Trail. Almost immediately turn sharp left on a narrow trail through the bamboo. As the trail begins to climb, turn right on an obscure trail leading straight down into the crater.

'Aihualama-'Ōhi'a has a lot of key junctions, some of which have signs. Memorize them for the return trip. On the Mānoa Cliff Trail watch for the junction with the Pu'u 'Ōhi'a Trail. You can easily walk right by it. (I did!) The various trails making up this hike receive regular maintenance. They are usually open and well groomed.

The Pauoa Flats Trail is also part of the Nu'uanu-Judd and Makiki-Tantalus hikes described in this book.

8 Makiki-Tantalus

Type:	Foothill
Length:	8 mi loop
Elev. Gain:	1,500 ft
Danger:	Low
Suitable for:	Novice, Intermediate
Location:	Leeward Koʻolau Range above Makiki
Topo Map:	Honolulu
Access:	Open

Trailhead Directions

Get on S. King St. Koko Head bound (east).

Turn left on Keʻeaumoku St.

After going over the freeway, turn right on Wilder Ave.

Take the first left on Makiki St.

After crossing Nehoa St. at the first traffic light, bear left on Makiki Heights Dr.

As the road switchbacks to the left, continue straight on an unnamed one-lane paved road.

Enter the Makiki Recreation Area.

Pass Hawaii Nature Center on the right.

Park on the side of the road just before a chain blocks further progress or park in the two lots on the right by the rest rooms (map point A).

Route Description

Continue along the road on foot, going around the chain.

Pass through a State Forestry base yard.

The pavement ends, and the road narrows to the Kanealole Trail.

Ascend gradually next to Kanealole Stream.

Reach the junction with the Makiki Valley Trail (map point B). Turn left and up on it. (To the right the valley trail crosses the stream and contours to Round Top Dr.)

Climb steeply on two switchbacks.

At the third switchback reach a junction (map point C). Turn sharp right and up on the Nahuina Trail. (The valley trail continues straight, through a large fallen trunk, and eventually reaches Tantalus Dr.)

Contour along the side of the ridge, crossing a small gully.

Climb gradually on four switchbacks.

Reach the end of Nahuina Trail at Tantalus Dr. (map point D). Turn right on the paved road.

At the end of the stone wall on the left bear left on the Mānoa Cliff Trail (map point E). (The one-lane paved road just to the right of the trail leads up to the top of Tantalus.)

Contour along the flank of Tantalus, working in and out of several gulches.

Pass a wooden bench on the left.

Reach a junction (map point F). Continue straight on the connector trail to Pauoa Flats. (The cliff trail curves right and contours around Tantalus.)

The path becomes rocky and rooty, but soon enters Pauoa Flats.

On the far side of the flats reach the junction with the Pauoa Flats Trail, which angles in from the right (map point G). Bear left on it. (The flats trail to the right is the return portion of the loop.)

Almost immediately reach another junction. Continue straight. (To the left is the Nu'uanu Trail, which heads down into Nu'uanu Valley and connects with the Judd Trail.)

In a bamboo grove reach a third junction. Continue straight on the flats trail. (To the right is the 'Aihualama Trail, which leads down to Mānoa Falls.)

Reach the Nu'uanu Valley overlook (elev. 1,600 ft) (map point H). (From there a rough trail continues to the summit of Kōnāhuanui. However, that trail is closed to the public because it goes through the Honolulu watershed.)

Retrace your steps past the 'Aihualama and Nu'uanu junctions to the junction with the connector trail (map point G). Now bear left, continuing on the flats trail.

Climb steeply up the side of Tantalus on a rocky eroded path.

Reach the junction with the Mānoa Cliff Trail (map point I). Turn left on it. (To the right the cliff trail heads back to Tantalus Dr.)

Reach another junction. Continue straight on the cliff trail. (To the right the Pu'u 'Ōhi'a Trail leads to the top of Tantalus.)

Contour around Tantalus, working in and out of several small gulches.

Pass an unnamed bench on the left and the Mānoa Cliff Bamboo Rest Bench on the right.

The Mānoa Cliff Trail ends at a switchback. Turn right and up on the connector trail to Round Top Dr. (map point J).

Ascend briefly to a broad ridge and then descend into a small gulch.

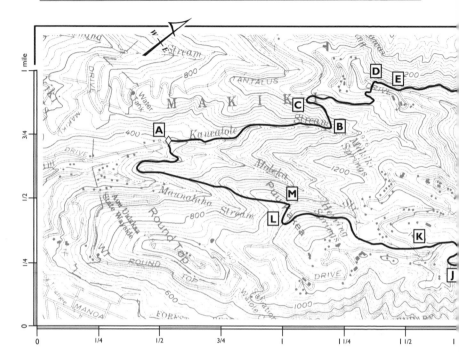

Reach the floor of the gulch and bear left down it as the trail widens.

Cross paved Round Top Dr. and pick up the Moleka Trail by a vehicle turnout (map point K).

Descend gradually, paralleling Moleka Stream, but well above it.

Climb briefly on two switchbacks up the side of Pu'u Kākea.

Reach the junction with the Makiki Valley Trail (map point L). Turn right on it. (To the left the valley trail contours back to Round Top Dr.)

Reach the junction with the 'Ualaka'a and Maunalaha Trails (map point M). Take the latter by bearing slightly left and down. (The 'Ualaka'a Trail requires a sharp left and leads to Round Top Dr. To the right is the continuation of the valley trail, which contours to Tantalus Dr.)

Descend steeply through eucalyptus, first on the left side of the ridge and then on the ridge line itself.

Bear right off the ridge line.

Descend the slope on two switchbacks.

Cross Kanealole Stream on a bridge.

Reach the rest rooms and the parking lots near the base yard (map point A).

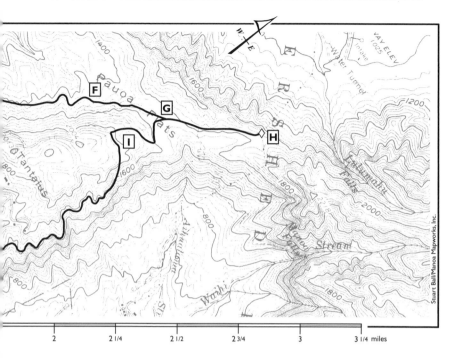

Notes

Makiki-Tantalus is a grand sightseeing trip on Oʻahu's best developed trail system. The hike incorporates parts of seven of the 11 trails in the Makiki-Tantalus complex. Although not crowded, the trails are well used because of their easy access and good condition.

This hike has numerous key junctions, some of which have signs. Follow the narrative closely. You can, of course, do the loop in the opposite direction if you don't mind reading the route description in reverse.

From the Nuʻuanu overlook you can see the Pali flanked by the peaks of Lanihuli on the left and Kōnāhuanui on the right. At 3,150 ft, the latter is the highest in the Koʻolau Range. Below is Nuʻuanu Valley with its reservoir. The Waiʻanae Range is in the distance to the left. There are good views of Mānoa Valley on the way back.

The various trails on this hike receive regular maintenance. They are usually open and well kept.

The Pauoa Flats Trail is also part of the ʻAihualama-ʻŌhiʻa and Nuʻuanu-Judd hikes.

9 Nuʻuanu-Judd

Type:	Foothill
Length:	5 mi round trip
Elev. Gain:	1,000 ft
Danger:	Low
Suitable for:	Novice, Intermediate
Location:	Leeward Koʻolau Range above Nuʻuanu
Topo Map:	Honolulu
Access:	Open

Trailhead Directions

At Punchbowl St. get on the Pali Hwy (Rte 61 north) heading up Nuʻuanu Valley.

Pass Queen Emma Summer Palace on the right and Oʻahu Country Club on the left.

Bear right on Nuʻuanu Pali Dr.

As the road forks, keep right, still on Nuʻuanu Pali Dr.

Cross a stream on a stone bridge.

Pass Polihiwa Pl. and then several houses on the left.

Look for a small bridge marked 1931 spanning a reservoir spillway.

Park in the small dirt lot just before the bridge (map point A).

Route Description

From the parking lot descend to Nuʻuanu Stream on the Judd Trail.

Cross the stream immediately upon reaching it. (Do not take the trail heading downstream along the near bank.)

Follow the wide trail heading away from the stream through a bamboo grove. Ignore the side trails along the stream.

Bear right along the slope.

Climb gradually through eucalyptus and Norfolk Island pines. Again, ignore the side trails heading upslope or down to the stream.

Enter the Charles S. Judd Memorial Grove of Norfolk Island pines.

As the trail descends, bear left into a shallow gully. The turn is marked by a short metal stake.

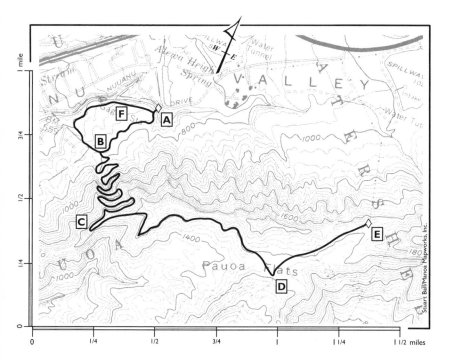

Cross the gully and bear right paralleling it.

Almost immediately reach the junction with the Nu'uanu Trail (map point B). Turn left and up on it. (The Judd loop continues straight downhill and is the route on the return.)

Ascend gradually up the side of Nu'uanu Valley on 25 (count 'em) switchbacks. After the fourteenth, pass a rock face on the right. After the eighteenth, leave the Norfolk Island pines behind. After the twenty-second, pass another rock face. After the twenty-third, cross a tiny waterfall chute.

After passing a banyan tree, reach the top of the ridge (map point C).

Turn left up it and climb steeply.

As the ridge levels momentarily in a small clearing, bear right off the ridge line on a grassy trail.

Begin contouring along the right side of the ridge.

Descend gradually toward Pauoa Flats, regaining the ridge line briefly.

The trail widens as it enters the flats.

Reach the end of the Nu'uanu Trail at its junction with the Pauoa Flats Trail (map point D). Turn left. (To the right the flats trail connects with the Mānoa Cliff Trail.)

In a bamboo grove reach the junction with the 'Aihualama Trail. Continue straight on the flats trail. (To the right the 'Aihualama Trail leads down to Mānoa Falls.)

Reach the Nu'uanu Valley overlook (elev. 1,600 ft) (map point E). (From there a rough trail continues to the summit of Kōnāhuanui. However, that trail is closed to the public because it goes through the Honolulu watershed.)

Retrace your steps along the Pauoa Flats and Nu'uanu Trails.

At the junction with the Judd Trail turn left to complete the loop (map point B).

Keep to the right while descending the ridge in a series of gentle switch-backs.

Cross two gullies with hau groves.

Swing to the right and contour well above Nu'uanu Stream.

Where the trail forks, bear left toward the stream. The fork is marked by a small metal stake.

Descend briefly on a rough trail to Jackass Ginger pool (map point F).

Climb back up from the pool and turn left on a makeshift trail heading upstream.

Pass a large banyan tree on the far bank.

Reach the initial stream crossing by the bamboo grove.

Turn left, cross Nu'uanu Stream, and climb the bank to the parking lot (map point A).

Notes

There are several easier ways to get to the Nu'uanu Valley overlook. The route described, however, is the most scenic and provides some good exercise. The less ambitious can just do the Judd loop.

From the Nu'uanu overlook you can see the Pali flanked by the peaks of Lanihuli on the left and Kōnāhuanui on the right. At 3,150 ft the latter is the highest in the Ko'olau Range. Below is Nu'uanu Valley with its reservoir. The Wai'anae Range is in the distance to the left. From the upper section of the Nu'uanu Trail you can look up to Tantalus and down into Punchbowl.

On the way back, stop off at Jackass Ginger for a cooling dip. The pool is very popular with local kids.

There are some mosquitoes along Nu'uanu Stream.

The two trails making up this hike receive regular maintenance. As a result, they are usually open and well groomed. The Nu'uanu Trail was completed in the fall of 1991.

The Pauoa Flats Trail is also part of the 'Aihualama-'Ōhi'a and Makiki-Tantalus hikes.

Leeward Ko'olau Range

KALIHI TO HĀLAWA

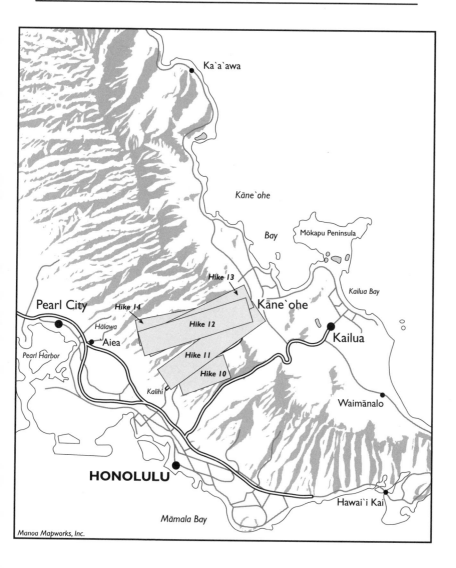

Ka`a`awa

Kāne`ohe

Bay

Mōkapu Peninsula

Hike 13

Kailua Bay

Pearl City

Hike 14

Kāne`ohe

Hālawa

Hike 12

Aiea

Kailua

Pearl Harbor

Hike 11

Kalihi

Hike 10

Waimānalo

HONOLULU

Hawai`i Kai

Māmala Bay

Manoa Mapworks, Inc.

10 Kamanaiki

Type:	Ungraded ridge
Length:	5 mi round trip
Elev. Gain:	1,300 ft
Danger:	Low
Suitable for:	Novice, Intermediate
Location:	Leeward Koʻolau Range above Kalihi
Topo Map:	Honolulu
Access:	Open

Trailhead Directions

At Punchbowl St. get on the Lunalilo Fwy (H-1) heading ʻewa (west).

Take Likelike Hwy (exit 20A, Rte 63 north) up Kalihi Valley.

At the fifth traffic light, by the pedestrian overpass, turn right on Nalaniʻeha St.

Cross Kalihi Stream on a bridge.

Park on the street near the intersection with Kalihi St. (map point A).

Route Description

Turn left on Kalihi St. by the Kalihi Uka pumping station.

Almost immediately turn right on Manaiki Pl.

At the road end take the concrete stairway straight ahead between two houses (map point B). It's just to the left of a utility pole.

Climb steeply on the stairs to the ridge line.

Bear left on a trail heading up the ridge through an ironwood grove.

Ascend three more flights of stairs to a water tank (map point C).

Keep the tank on the left and continue up the ridge through ironwoods.

Break out into the open and climb a steep hill.

Pass through a large eucalyptus forest with another uphill section.

Cross another open, grassy area.

Reach a small knob marked by an eroded cliff on the left (map point D).

Traverse a narrow windswept section covered with Christmas berry.

Reach a second, less distinct knob (map point E).

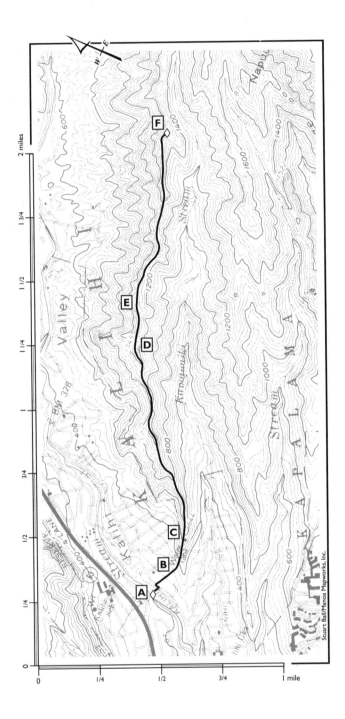

Continue along the ridge top to a small ironwood grove.

Traverse another windswept section.

Climb steeply to a flat-topped hill. A cable is provided for assistance at the steepest part.

Enter the native rain forest dominated by koa and 'ōhi'a trees and uluhe ferns.

Climb gradually through the uluhe.

Reach a small clearing (elev. 1,560 ft) marked by a large, partially fallen koa tree (map point F). On the right is an uluhe-covered side ridge. There are commanding views of Kalihi Valley and the rest of the ridge.

Notes

This hike leads partway up the ridge between Kalihi and Kamanaiki valleys. It provides a good introduction to ridge hiking on O'ahu. The trail is easy to follow; however, there are some steep climbs and narrow sections. Novices should go as far as feels comfortable and then turn around.

From the clearing at the end are good views of Kalihi Valley on the left and Kamanaiki Valley on the right. Lanihuli is the massive mountain ahead between the Wilson Tunnel and the Pali.

The trail receives sporadic maintenance. The lower section is usually open, but the upper section overgrows between clearings.

11 Bowman

Type:	Ungraded ridge
Length:	12 mi round trip
Elev. Gain:	2,400 ft
Danger:	Medium
Suitable for:	Intermediate, Expert
Location:	Leeward Koʻolau Range above Fort Shafter
Topo Map:	Honolulu, Kāneʻohe
Access:	Open

Trailhead Directions

At Punchbowl St. get on the Lunalilo Fwy (H-1) heading ʻewa (west).

Take Likelike Hwy (exit 20A, Rte 63 north) up Kalihi Valley.

At the fifth traffic light, by the pedestrian overpass, turn left on Nālaniʻeha St.

At its end, turn left on Kula Kōlea Dr.

At the next intersection turn right on Nāʻai St.

Park on the street near its end (map point A).

Route Description

Continue along Nāʻai St. on foot.

At its end by Kalihi Elementary School, turn left on Hālina St.

Just before it ends at a water tank, turn right into the school playing field and head for the basketball courts.

Between the red and yellow backboards turn left up the side of the ridge on a trail (map point B).

Cross a low retaining wall.

Ascend straight up toward a utility pole.

At the pole bear left and contour briefly.

Resume steep climbing, first through an open area, and then through mixed ironwoods and Christmas berry.

The trail levels off somewhat through an ironwood grove. Keep to the left in this section.

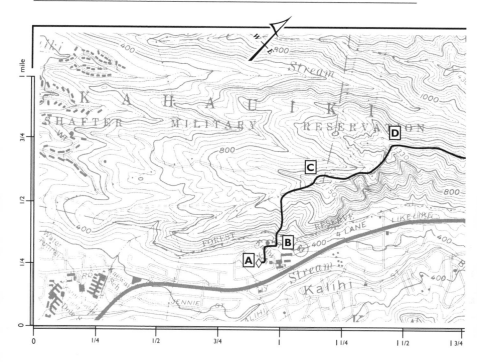

Leave the ironwoods for an open grassy area.

Reach a dirt road by some utility lines and turn right on it.

Climb steeply on the road following the utility lines.

At the crest of the ridge reach a junction with Radar Hill Rd. (map point C). Turn right on it. (To the left the road is semipaved and leads down to Fort Shafter.)

The dirt road skirts a hump in the ridge, dips, and then climbs steeply to the left.

At the ridge top turn right, off the road just before a power-line tower.

Reach the start of the Bowman Trail behind a small concrete building on the right (map point D).

Keep left while descending briefly through an ironwood grove.

Pass United States Military Reservation (USMR) marker no. 22 on the left.

Enter a long stretch of guava.

Pass marker no. 21 on the right at the top of a hill (map point E).

An opening nearby provides a view of the entire ridge to be climbed.

Cross a level section through mixed exotic forest.

Climb briefly to a second hill with two rocks on top.

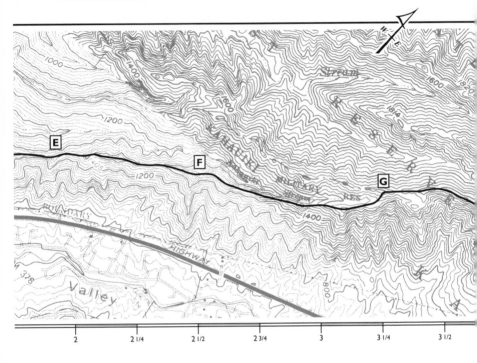

Enter the native rain forest with koa trees and uluhe ferns.

Ascend gradually to a third hill with marker no. 20 on the right (map point F).

Come abreast of the last house in Kalihi Valley.

Traverse a series of short, steep descents, passing marker no. 19 on the left.

Cross a narrow, but level, section, inching to the right of a rock face.

Ascend steeply with the aid of a cable.

Pass marker no. 18 on the left in an ironwood grove.

Climb gradually to marker no. 17 at the top of a hill and then descend through ironwoods.

Climb steeply through uluhe to reach the junction of the two ridges forming the head of Kahauiki Valley (map point G). Bear right to continue to the Koʻolau summit.

Begin climbing gradually toward Puʻu Kahuauli.

Under a spreading koa tree reach a junction. Continue straight along the main ridge on the grassy trail. (The faint trail down the side ridge to the right leads to Likelike Hwy.)

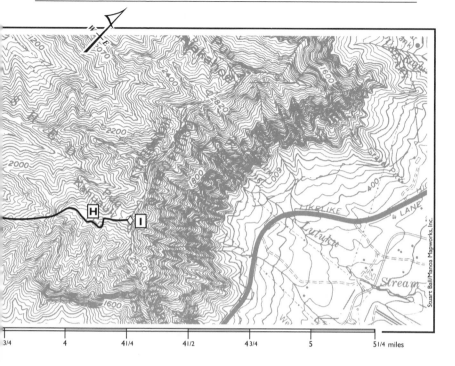

3/4   4   4 1/4   4 1/2   4 3/4   5   5 1/4 miles

Bear right to contour around a hump in the ridge.

Past the hump turn sharp left up a side ridge.

Climb very steeply with the aid of a cable.

Bear left across the face of the hump (map point H).

Switchback once to regain the main ridge. Once again cables are provided for the narrow sections.

The ridge broadens, and the trail becomes quite muddy.

Climb a small grassy gully with exposed rock on the right.

At the end of the gully turn right along the ridge.

Bear left, following the ridge.

Reach the Koʻolau summit at Puʻu Kahuauli (elev. 2,740 ft) (map point I).

Notes

Bowman is the most difficult of the ungraded ridge hikes in the leeward Koʻolau Range. It starts with a stiff climb, traverses a long stretch of ups and downs and culminates in the spectacular climb of Puʻu Kahuauli. The only detraction is the noise from vehicles on Likelike Hwy below.

The complete trip is for advanced hikers only. Intermediate hikers can go as far as they like. Novices should get some experience on easier hikes before trying this one.

On the way up (down) are good views of Honolulu, Pearl Harbor, and the Wai'anae Range in the distance. From the top you can see the windward coast from Waimānalo to Kāne'ohe Bay.

Turn left along the Ko'olau summit to reach the Tripler Ridge and Pu'u Keahi a Kahoe hikes. This stretch is relatively easy as summit hiking goes, but it's still for experienced walkers only. Up Bowman and down Tripler Ridge or either portion of the Keahi a Kahoe loop makes an outstanding trip.

Be especially careful on the narrow sections. In many cases they are masked by low vegetation and are thus doubly dangerous. Test all cables before using them.

The trails making up this hike receive periodic maintenance. The middle and upper sections of the Bowman Trail overgrow between clearings. The ridge access trail and the lower section of Bowman are usually open.

Some of the strawberry guavas in the lower section are the yellow variety, which is more tasty, but less common, than the red one. The yellow guava usually ripens in August and September.

Access is also available from Radar Hill Rd. in Fort Shafter. However, written permission is required from the Directorate of Facilities Engineering, U.S. Army Support Command, Fort Shafter, HI 96858.

12 Tripler Ridge

Type:	Ungraded ridge
Length:	11 mi round trip
Elev. Gain:	2,100 ft
Danger:	Low
Suitable for:	Novice, Intermediate, Expert
Location:	Leeward Ko'olau Range above Tripler Hospital
Topo Map:	Honolulu, Kāne'ohe
Access:	Conditional; open to outdoor clubs and organizations with permission. Contact the Directorate of Facilities Engineering, U.S. Army Support Command, Fort Shafter, HI 96858, and Moanalua Gardens, 1352 Pineapple Pl., Honolulu, HI 96819 (phone 833–1944).

Trailhead Directions

At Punchbowl St. get on the Lunalilo Fwy (H-1) heading 'ewa (west).

Near Middle St. keep left on Rte 78 west (exit 19B, Moanalua Rd.) to 'Aiea.

Take the exit marked Pu'uloa Rd.—Tripler Hospital.

At the top of the off ramp turn right on Jarrett White Rd.

Pass a guard station on the right and enter Tripler Army Medical Center.

Just past the hospital bear right, still on Jarrett White Rd.

Pass a heliport on the left.

At the end of the road turn right on Krukowski Rd. in the back of a military housing area.

Take the first left on a one-lane semipaved road.

Park on the side of the road near its intersection with another paved road on the left (map point A).

Route Description

Walk up the one-lane paved road on the left with the chain across it.

Climb steadily along the broad ridge through mixed guava and Christmas berry.

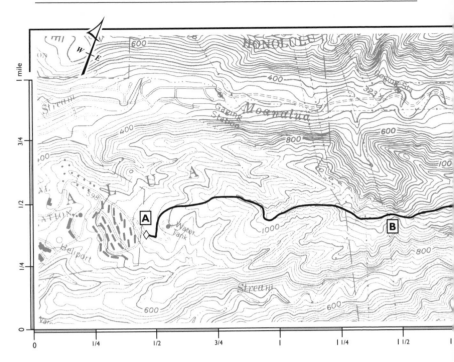

On the left pass a dirt road heading off the ridge.

Reach a radar installation at the end of the paved road.

Continue straight on a dirt road that goes under several power lines.

Bear left and descend briefly to a power-line tower, where the road ends (map point B).

At the far side of the tower pick up the Tripler Ridge Trail, which continues along the ridge through dense stands of guava.

Work right, around a large knob in the ridge.

Ascend gradually to a second knob with a tall Norfolk Island pine on top (map point C).

Cross a level eroded stretch.

Climb another hump in the ridge (map point D). While descending its back side, keep left around a steep eroded section. There is a cable for assistance.

Proceed over a series of small knobs through more guava.

Enter the native rain forest dominated by koa trees and uluhe ferns.

Ascend sharply to a large hump (map point E) and then traverse a relatively level section.

Climb another large knob (map point F).

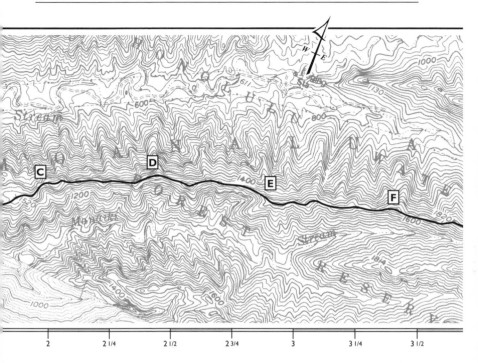

Pass a recent landslide on the left.

Begin the long climb to the summit.

Negotiate a particularly steep, narrow section.

Reach a junction just before a small flat clearing marked by a metal pipe (map point G). Continue straight along the main ridge. (To the left is an old Hawaiian Electric access trail that leads down into Moanalua Valley. That trail is part of the Pu'u Keahi a Kahoe loop, as is the remainder of this hike.)

Climb steeply to a sharp peak (false summit!).

Cross a short level stretch.

Ascend gradually over several small humps.

Reach the Ko'olau summit at a flat-topped peak (elev. 2,760 ft) (map point H). To the left is a power-line tower.

Notes

Tripler Ridge is a classic leeward Ko'olau ridge hike. It's long, hard, and somewhat tedious, but it finishes with a bang. The trail first passes through endless stands of guava. It then enters the rain forest with a good variety of native plants. Finally, the trail emerges onto the open windswept slopes near

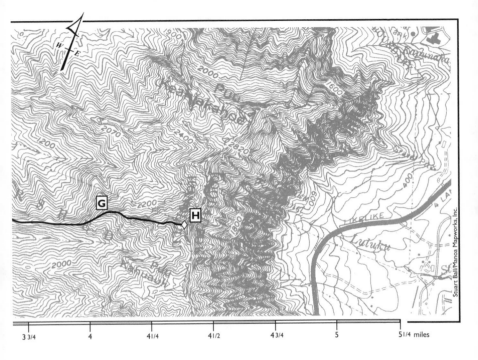

3 3/4   4   4 1/4   4 1/2   4 3/4   5   5 1/4 miles

the summit. The last mile provides some of the finest ridge walking on the island.

The entire route is for experienced hikers only. However, novices and intermediates can go as far as they like and then turn around.

From the top you can see Kāne'ohe Bay and town and much of the windward coast. The view to leeward encompasses Honolulu, the Wahiawā plain, and the Wai'anae Range in the distance.

Turn right along the summit for a short jaunt to Bowman. Turn left to reach the summit of Pu'u Keahi a Kahoe. That wild windy stretch is described in the Pu'u Keahi a Kahoe narrative. Up Tripler and down Bowman or either portion of the Pu'u Keahi a Kahoe loop makes a superb outing for expert hikers.

The trail receives sporadic maintenance. The middle section overgrows quickly between clearings. The lower and upper sections are comparatively open.

The strawberry guavas along the trail are the yellow variety, which is delicious. They ripen in August and September.

13 Pu'u Keahi a Kahoe

Type:	Ungraded ridge
Length:	11 mi loop
Elev. Gain:	2,600 ft
Danger:	High
Suitable for:	Intermediate, Expert
Location:	Leeward Ko'olau Range above Moanalua
Topo Map:	Kāne'ohe
Access:	Conditional; open to individuals and organized groups with permission. Contact Moanalua Gardens, 1352 Pineapple Pl., Honolulu, HI 96819 (phone 833-1944).

Trailhead Directions

At Punchbowl St. get on the Lunalilo Fwy (H-1) heading 'ewa (west).

Near Middle St. keep left on Rte 78 west (exit 19B, Moanalua Rd.) to 'Aiea.

Take the exit marked Moanalua Valley—Red Hill.

From the off ramp turn right on Ala Aolani St. heading into Moanalua Valley.

The road ends at Moanalua Valley Park.

Park on the street just before the park entrance (map point A).

Route Description

Enter Moanalua Valley Park and proceed along the dirt/gravel road at the back of the parking lot.

Walk around a locked gate to the right.

On the left by a huge monkeypod tree pass a muddy driveway leading to the Douglas Damon house site.

Cross Moanalua Stream seven times on stone bridges.

To the right at the seventh crossing is a large boulder covered with petroglyphs (map point B). It is called Pōhaku Luahine (rock of the old woman).

Around the bend from the petroglyph rock and before the next stream

49

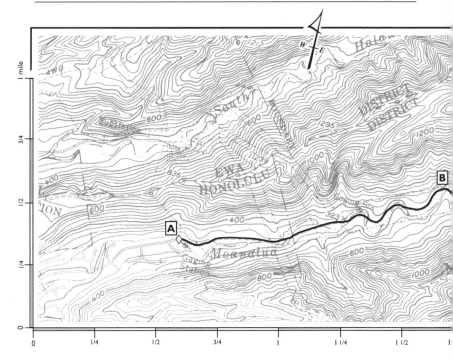

crossing is a short loop trail to the right. It climbs up to the May Damon house site.

Ford the stream 10 times. After the fourth crossing ascend gradually to a wide vehicle turnaround area (map point C). There an eroded dirt road on the right leads up to an overlook of the entire valley.

After the tenth crossing and as the road curves right, reach an obscure junction (map point D). It is marked by a koa tree with a vertical blaze cut long ago. Continue along the road. (The trail to the left crosses the stream and then forks. To the right, up the middle ridge, is the return portion of the Pu'u Keahi a Kahoe loop. To the left a trail follows the left fork of the stream.)

Cross the stream once again (no. 11).

The road becomes narrower and more rutted as it climbs toward the back of the valley.

Just before the twelfth ford, bear left on a grassy road (map point E). (The main road ends in an open area just after the crossing.)

The grassy road quickly narrows to a trail.

Ascend gradually beside the stream through mixed forest and ginger.

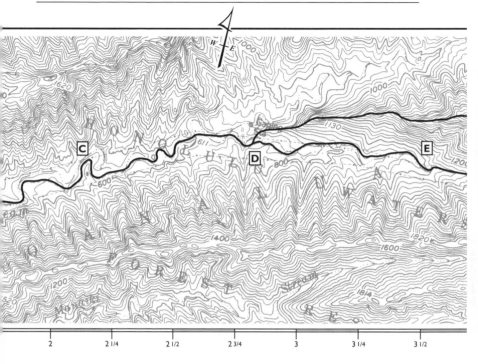

Cross the main stream channel to a small island.

Walk upstream on the island for a short distance and then cross the secondary channel.

Climb straight up briefly, then bear left to ascend steadily along the side of the valley.

Cross the top of a tiny waterfall chute.

Continue to ascend on two short and then two longer switchbacks.

Climb straight up the ridge. The footing is very loose and slippery.

Bear right and then switchback two more times.

Pass two wire supports for some power-line poles above.

Switchback once more and then climb to a cleared spot just above the poles (map point F).

Turn sharp right and climb straight up the side ridge.

Pass a power-line tower.

Reach the ridge top and the junction with the Tripler Ridge Trail (map point G). Turn left on it up the ridge. (To the right the trail leads down Tripler Ridge toward the hospital.)

Climb steeply to a false summit.

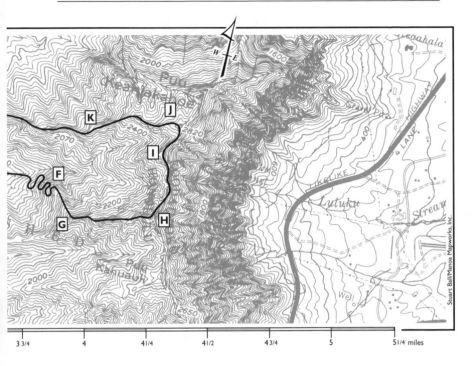

Traverse a short level section and then begin the final ascent to the top.

Reach the Ko'olau summit at a flat grassy knob (elev. 2,760 ft) (map point H).

Turn left along the summit, passing a power-line tower.

Descend steeply on the narrow ridge.

Cross a level section marked by several metal posts.

Reach a junction where the posts diverge. Keep left and up following the red posts.

Pass a lone metal rod on the left.

Walk under another large tower.

Bear left around the embankment on the far side of the tower.

Climb steeply past an abandoned radar.

Reach the top of a peak (map point I) and descend its back side, still on the summit ridge.

Traverse a relatively level, but extremely narrow and rough section.

Ascend very steeply on grass, keeping to the edge of the ridge.

Reach the flat summit of Pu'u Keahi a Kahoe (elev. 2,820 ft) (map point J), which is identified by a benchmark.

There the trail splits. Take the left fork, which heads down the middle ridge of Moanalua Valley. (The right fork continues a short distance along the summit to the top of Ha'ikū Stairs.)

The ridge narrows and is severely windswept.

The ridge widens briefly (map point K). Keep to the left to avoid going down a side ridge.

Descend steeply, bear right, and then descend very steeply.

Descend leisurely on the broad ridge as the vegetation thickens.

Pass a small landslide on the right.

Descend a short steep section and then ascend a short rocky one.

Continue to descend through strawberry guava and then uluhe ferns.

Pass a large sandalwood tree on the right.

Descend through uluhe again and then guava.

Cross Moanalua Stream just above the obscure junction of the road and the stream trail (map point D).

Turn right on the dirt road.

Retrace your steps to Moanalua Valley Park (map point A).

Notes

Pu'u Keahi a Kahoe is the mist-shrouded peak at the back of Moanalua Valley. The hike starts and finishes with a pleasant valley stroll. In between is a walk on the wild side. If you are an experienced hiker, try the entire loop and see why it's known as a "wow" hike. Intermediates can take the middle ridge to the summit and then return the same way.

Pu'u Keahi a Kahoe earns its expert rating and then some. It is one of only a handful of hikes in this book that go along the Ko'olau summit. There are numerous narrow and steep spots on the loop portion. Often they are masked by vegetation and so are doubly dangerous. Walk gingerly along the narrow windswept summit.

The views on this hike are spectacular. From the top the pali drops 2,000 ft almost straight down. You can see the windward coast from Kāne'ohe to Waimānalo bays. Kāne'ohe and Kailua towns are in front. The triple-peaked mountain in the distance to the right is Olomana. On the way down the whole of Moanalua Valley spreads out before you. In the distance are Pearl Harbor and the Wai'anae Range.

Turn right along the summit to reach the Bowman Trail. That stretch is relatively easy, as summit hiking goes. You can make up several combination trips using the Pu'u Keahi a Kahoe, Tripler Ridge, or Bowman hikes and connecting them along the summit.

The trails used on this hike receive periodic maintenance. The lower section of the middle ridge and the switchback trail overgrow between clearings.

There is a good variety of native plants along the summit and down the middle ridge.

Along the road after the turnaround is a grove of the yellow variety of strawberry guava. It is more tasty, but less common, than the red variety. The yellow variety usually ripens in September.

Moanalua Valley is rich in historical sites and legends. Take the informative hike/tour offered by the Moanalua Gardens Foundation.

The Ha'ikū Stairs is a metal ladder/stairway that leads straight down the cliffs to the U.S. Coast Guard Omega Station in Ha'ikū Valley. The stairs are currently closed because of missing sections and general deterioration.

The Pu'u Keahi a Kahoe hike includes portions of other hikes. The Moanalua Valley hike shares the dirt road and then turns off on to the stream trail. The Tripler Ridge hike starts back of the hospital and then shares the upper section of Tripler Ridge.

14 Moanalua Valley

Type:	Valley
Length:	11 mi round trip
Elev. Gain:	1,400 ft
Danger:	Low
Suitable for:	Novice, Intermediate
Location:	Leeward Koʻolau Range above Moanalua
Topo Map:	Kāneʻohe
Access:	Conditional; open to individuals and organized groups with permission. Contact Moanalua Gardens, 1352 Pineapple Pl., Honolulu, HI 96819 (phone 833–1944).

Trailhead Directions

At Punchbowl St. get on the Lunalilo Fwy (H-1) heading ʻewa (west).

Near Middle St. keep left on Rte 78 west (exit 19B, Moanalua Rd.) to ʻAiea.

Take the exit marked Moanalua Valley—Red Hill.

From the off ramp turn right on Ala Aolani St. heading into Moanalua Valley.

The road ends at Moanalua Valley Park.

Park on the street just before the park entrance (map point A).

Route Description

Enter Moanalua Valley Park and proceed along the dirt/gravel road at the back of the parking lot.

Walk around a locked gate to the right.

On the left by a huge monkeypod tree pass a muddy driveway leading to the Douglas Damon house site (marker no. 3).

Cross Moanalua Stream seven times on stone bridges.

To the right at the seventh crossing is a large boulder covered with petroglyphs (map point B) (marker no. 10). It is called Pōhaku Luahine (rock of the old woman).

Around the bend from the petroglyph rock and before the next stream

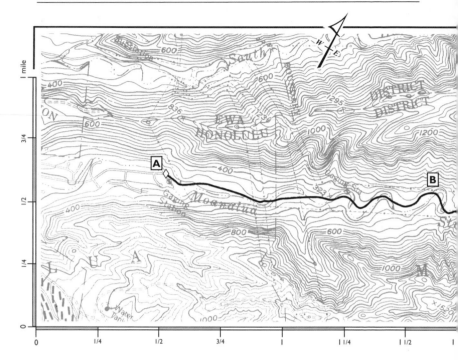

crossing is a short loop trail to the right (marker no. 11). It climbs up to the May Damon house site.

Ford the stream 10 times. After the fourth crossing ascend gradually to a wide vehicle turnaround area (map point C) (marker no. 13). There, an eroded dirt road on the right leads up to an overlook of the entire valley.

After the tenth crossing and as the road curves right, look for a koa tree with a long vertical blaze cut long ago.

At the marked tree turn left off the road on to a trail (map point D). (The road continues to the back of the valley.)

Cross the stream immediately, climb the embankment, and reach a junction. Turn left. (The trail to the right leads up the middle ridge.)

Skirt the foot of the middle ridge, which divides the valley into two drainages.

Pass a stream gauging station on the left.

Cross the stream 23 times! Highlights are as follows: At 6: a small, but delightful pool. Just after the pool is another petroglyph rock on the right. At 8: a dense hau grove. Between 12 and 13: Climb over a small side ridge and then descend steeply back to the stream. Between 14 and 15: a dense hau grove. Keep your head down! After 18: Break out into the open for a short

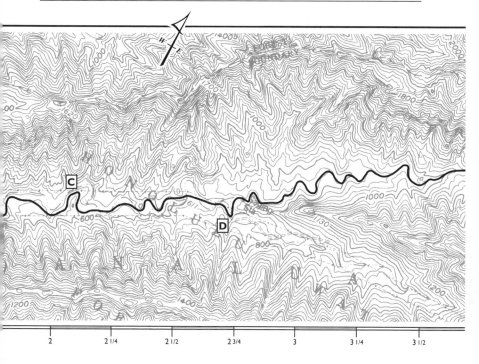

stretch. After 20: another hau tangle. The stream then splits in two several times. The trail generally hugs the main (left) channel on the islands created by the two braids. At 21: a tiny pool and waterfall.

After the twenty-third crossing, leave the stream for good and begin the final ascent (map point E).

Climb steeply up a spur ridge through uluhe ferns.

Reach the Ko'olau summit at a saddle (elev. 1,680 ft) (map point F).

Notes

Moanalua is a classic valley hike. It offers some easy road walking, a lovely stream trail, and a short ridge climb at the end.

From the top you can look straight down into Ha'ikū Valley. The cluster of buildings below is the U.S. Coast Guard Omega Station. The Ha'ikū Stairs are visible on the steep side ridge to the right. Along the coast is Kāne'ohe Bay and town.

The junction with the stream trail is not obvious. Keep track of the stream crossings on the road, and you should be able to find the junction. It may be marked with surveyor's ribbon, but don't count on it.

The stream trail is occasionally obscure, especially in areas where pigs have

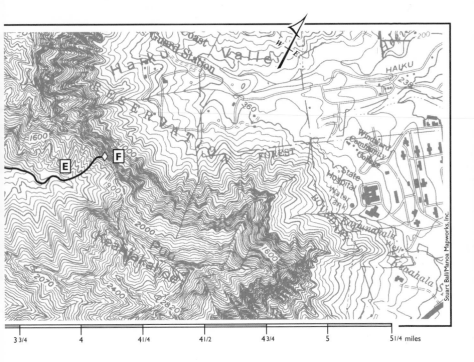

been rooting. If you lose your way, just follow the stream, and you will pick up the trail shortly.

Watch your footing while crossing the stream. The rocks can be very slippery. Eventually your boots are going to get wet, anyway.

On the way down, stop at the small pool near the sixth crossing for a cool dip.

There are some mosquitoes along the stream.

The stream trail receives regular maintenance. Only the stretch of uluhe near the summit and some of the hau groves overgrow quickly between clearings. As a result, the trail is open for the most part, as is the dirt road.

A short side trip leads to the site of an old plane crash at the bottom of a high, but intermittent waterfall. To get there, leave the trail at the last stream crossing (no. 23) and walk up the stream bed. The wreckage of the plane is strewn along the stream just below the waterfall. At its base is a pleasant clearing with a tiny pool.

Moanalua Valley is rich in historical sites and legends. Take the informative hike/tour offered by the Moanalua Gardens Foundation. They will explain more fully the points of interest marked by the numbered wooden posts.

The dirt road into the valley is also part of the Pu'u Keahi a Kahoe hike.

ʻAIEA TO PEARL CITY

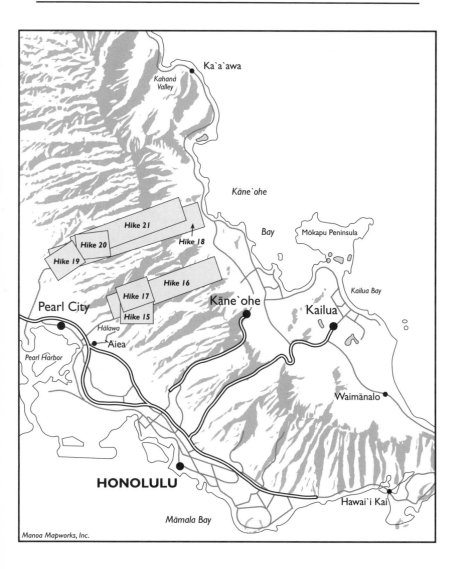

Ka`a`awa

Kahana
Valley

Kāne`ohe

Hike 21

Hike 20

Hike 19

Hike 18

Bay

Mōkapu Peninsula

Hike 16

Hike 17

Kāne`ohe

Hike 15

Kailua Bay

Pearl City

Kailua

Hālawa

`Aiea

Pearl Harbor

Waimānalo

HONOLULU

Hawai`i Kai

Māmala Bay

Manoa Mapworks, Inc.

15 'Aiea Loop

Type:	Foothill
Length:	5 mi loop
Elev. Gain:	900 ft
Danger:	Low
Suitable for:	Novice
Location:	Leeward Ko'olau Range above 'Aiea
Topo Map:	Waipahu, Kāne'ohe
Access:	Open

Trailhead Directions

At Punchbowl St. get on the Lunalilo Fwy (H-1) heading 'ewa (west).

Near Middle St. keep left on Rte 78 west (exit 19B, Moanalua Rd.) to 'Aiea.

While descending Red Hill, take the exit marked Stadium—Hālawa.

At the end of the long off ramp continue straight on Ulunē St.

At the road end turn right on 'Aiea Heights Dr.

Pass 'Aiea Sugar Mill on the right.

Climb gradually through 'Aiea Heights.

Reach the entrance to Keaīwa Heiau State Recreation Area.

Drive past the heiau and the camping area to the upper lot and park there (map point A).

Route Description

At the back of the upper lot take the 'Aiea Loop Trail.

Pass a small water tank on the right.

Enter a eucalyptus forest.

Cross an open eroded area with a view back toward Honolulu.

Pass a power-line tower above and to the right.

Shortly afterward reach a junction (map point B). Continue straight on the loop trail. (The trail to the left leads down to Kalauao Stream.)

Pass a second power-line tower on the right.

Contour on the right side of the ridge just below its top.

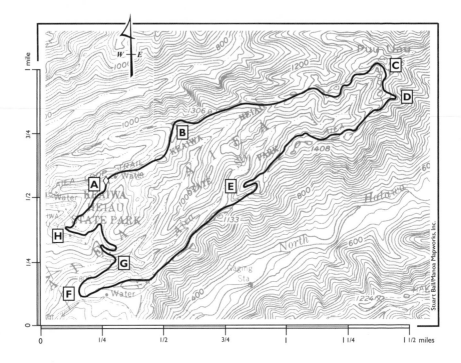

Reach a small grassy clearing with several stumps. From there is a good view of the Wai'anae Range in the distance.

Continue contouring well below the ridge line.

Step gingerly through a muddy spot where several logs span the trail. There are smaller logs imbedded in the path for more secure footing.

Right after the muddy spot the trail curves left and then right.

As it begins to curve right, reach another junction (map point C). Continue on the wide loop trail to the right. (The narrower trail to the left is the 'Aiea Ridge Trail, which leads to the Ko'olau summit.)

Cross over to the left side of the ridge. There are good views of the Ko'olau Range through the trees.

Reach the farthest point of the loop by a large 'ōhi'a tree with exposed roots (map point D).

Along the first part of the return leg are views of North Hālawa Valley on the left.

Switch to the right side of the ridge.

Descend gradually, well below the ridge line, through eucalyptus.

In a gully, pass the wing section of a C-47 cargo plane on the right. A steep trail leads to other wreckage farther down the gully. The plane crashed in 1943.

Pass a power-line tower above and to the left (map point E). Pass a second one.

Stroll through a grove of Norfolk Island pines on a broad trail.

Reach a junction. Keep right on the contour trail. (The eroded trail to the left climbs to a view of Honolulu and Salt Lake.)

Go under some power lines.

Pass another grove of Norfolk Island pines.

In a stand of albizia trees, reach another junction (map point F). Bear right on the wide trail. (The left fork leads to Camp Smith.)

Switchback once and descend into a gulch.

Cross the intermittent stream (map point G) and climb out of the gulch on a rocky, rooty trail with three switchbacks.

Switchback once again past a power-line tower on the left.

The trail levels off.

Enter the camping area of the park (map point H).

Turn right and climb the steps to the middle parking lot.

Turn right again and walk up the paved road to the upper parking lot (map point A).

Notes

It seems as if everyone who has ever hiked on O'ahu has done the 'Aiea Loop Trail. If you haven't, try it. It's a great hike for beginners. If you have, try some of the other novice hikes in this book.

The loop trail receives regular maintenance and is always open. The footpath is, for the most part, graded and wide. The only rough section is the short climb out of the gulch near the end of the hike.

Most of the vegetation on this hike is introduced. There are some large native koa and 'ōhi'a trees at the far end of the loop.

The return portion of the loop is sometimes used by horseback riders from Camp Smith. If you see horses, stand quietly off the trail and let them pass.

The strawberry guavas along the initial stretch usually ripen in August and September.

The initial section of this hike is also part of the Kalauao and 'Aiea Ridge hikes.

16 'Aiea Ridge

Type:	Ungraded ridge
Length:	11 mi round trip
Elev. Gain:	1,700 ft
Danger:	Low
Suitable for:	Novice, Intermediate, Expert
Location:	Leeward Ko'olau Range above 'Aiea
Topo Map:	Waipahu, Kāne'ohe
Access:	Open

Trailhead Directions

At Punchbowl St. get on the Lunalilo Fwy (H-1) heading 'ewa (west).

Near Middle St. keep left on Rte 78 west (exit 19B, Moanalua Rd.) to 'Aiea.

While descending Red Hill, take the exit marked Stadium—Hālawa.

At the end of the long off ramp continue straight on Ulunē St.

At the road end turn right on 'Aiea Heights Dr.

Pass 'Aiea Sugar Mill on the right.

Climb gradually through 'Aiea Heights.

Reach the entrance to Keaīwa Heiau State Recreation Area.

Drive past the heiau and the camping area to the upper lot and park there (map point A).

Route Description

At the back of the upper lot take the 'Aiea Loop Trail.

Pass a small water tank on the right.

Enter a eucalyptus forest.

Cross an open eroded area with a view back toward Honolulu.

Pass a power-line tower above and to the right.

Shortly afterward reach a junction (map point B). Continue straight on the loop trail. (The trail to the left leads down to Kalauao Stream.)

Pass a second power-line tower on the right.

Contour on the right side of the ridge just below its top.

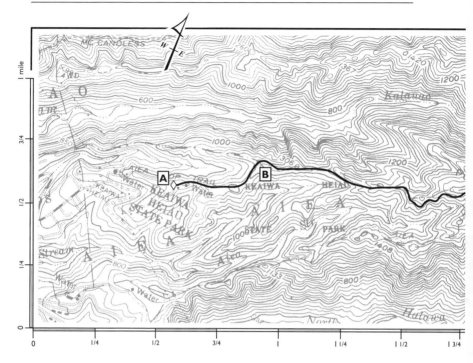

Reach a small grassy clearing with several stumps.

Continue contouring well below the ridge line.

Step gingerly through a muddy spot where several logs span the trail. There are smaller logs imbedded in the path for more secure footing.

Right after the muddy spot the trail curves left and then right.

As it begins to curve right, reach another junction (map point C). Turn left and up on the narrower 'Aiea Ridge Trail. (The wider loop trail continues to the right.)

Almost immediately reach the edge of the ridge and bear left.

Go around to the right of Pu'u 'U'au, a large hill on the ridge.

Regain the ridge top and traverse a relatively level, but rooty, section with some large koa trees.

Continue along the ridge, now with more ups and downs.

Walk under a large arch formed by a downed koa tree.

Contour along the right side of the ridge for a short distance.

Descend briefly, but steeply.

Climb gradually, skirting a large hill on the ridge (map point D).

Cross a partially open, level stretch.

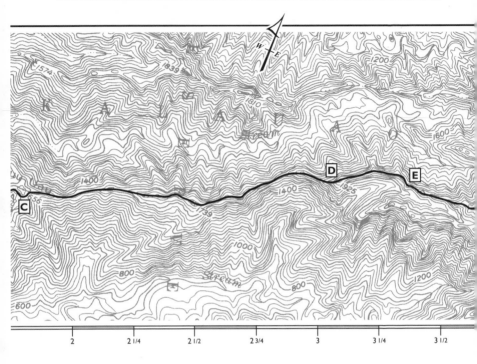

Descend to an open saddle on the ridge (map point E).

Begin the climb to Pu'u Kawipo'o, the large peak looming ahead.

Pass a small clearing on the right.

After a stiff ascent, reach the top of Pu'u Kawipo'o (elev. 2,441 ft) (map point F).

Climb gradually over a series of small humps. The ridge is open, windswept, and at times narrow.

Reach a large grassy clearing on the left with good views of the windward side (map point G).

Turn right and down, still on the main ridge, toward a power-line tower.

Bear left around the base of the tower.

Climb steadily along the ridge, which levels off near the top.

Reach the Ko'olau summit (elev. 2,805 ft) (map point H).

Notes

'Aiea Ridge is a gem of a ridge hike. The access is easy, and the trail is in pretty good shape. There are a number of different native plants in the middle and upper sections. You can see some native birds, too. The final stretch

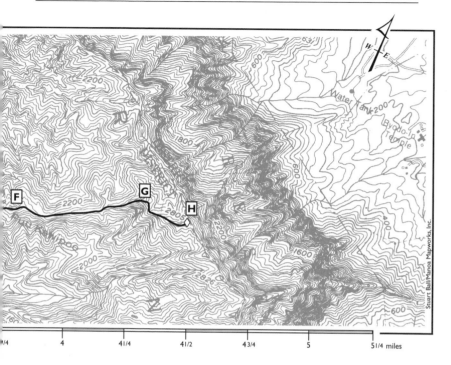

along the open ridge is wild and wonderful. Novices and intermediates can go as far as they like and then turn around.

From the top you can see all of Kāne'ohe Bay. To the right are Kāne'ohe town and the Marine Corps Air Station. The Wai'anae Range is in the distance to leeward.

The loop trail receives regular maintenance and is always open. The ridge trail receives periodic maintenance. The lower and middle sections overgrow between clearings. The wind keeps the vegetation low on the upper section.

The strawberry guavas on the loop trail usually ripen in August and September.

The initial section of this hike along the loop trail is also part of the Kalauao and 'Aiea Loop hikes.

17 Kalauao

Type:	Valley
Length:	4 mi round trip
Elev. Gain:	700 ft
Danger:	Low
Suitable for:	Novice, Intermediate
Location:	Leeward Koʻolau Range above ʻAiea
Topo Map:	Waipahu, Kāneʻohe
Access:	Open

Trailhead Directions

At Punchbowl St. get on the Lunalilo Fwy (H-1) heading ʻewa (west).

Near Middle St. keep left on Rte 78 west (exit 19B, Moanalua Rd.) to ʻAiea.

While descending Red Hill, take the exit marked Stadium—Hālawa.

At the end of the long off ramp continue straight on Ulunē St.

At the road end turn right on ʻAiea Heights Dr.

Pass ʻAiea Sugar Mill on the right.

Climb gradually through ʻAiea Heights.

Reach the entrance to Keaīwa Heiau State Recreation Area.

Drive past the heiau and the camping area to the upper lot and park there (map point A).

Route Description

At the back of the upper lot take the ʻAiea Loop Trail.

Pass a small water tank on the right.

Enter a eucalyptus forest.

Cross an open eroded area with a view back toward Honolulu.

Pass a power-line tower above and to the right.

The trail then curves to the right and then to the left.

After that S curve reach a junction (map point B). Turn left and down on a side trail. (The ʻAiea Loop Trail continues straight.)

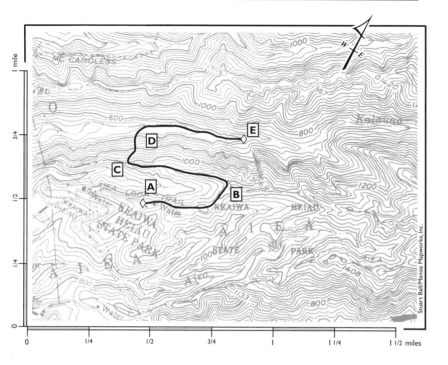

Descend gradually along the side ridge through strawberry guava.

Walk under a power-line tower.

The trail narrows through strawberry guava.

Pass a grove of paperbark trees.

In an open area with anemic-looking ironwoods bear right, still on the ridge top.

Go through a long corridor of ironwoods.

The trail widens through a grove of eucalyptus.

In the grove look for a small eroded area and a mango tree on the right.

At the mango tree reach a junction (map point C). Turn sharp right off the ridge on a narrow trail leading down into Kalauao Valley.

Pass some ironwoods on the right.

Descend steeply through Christmas berry trees.

Jog right and then left to avoid a rock face.

Resume the steep descent.

Reach Kalauao Stream and cross it (map point D). Turn right, heading upstream.

Cross the stream seven more times.

Just after the ninth crossing reach a delightful, if small, pool and waterfall (map point E).

Notes

If you have already done the 'Aiea Loop Trail, try this harder variation. It is a challenging novice hike because of the steep, rough descent into Kalauao Valley. The lovely pool and waterfall at the end, however, make it all worthwhile.

The stream section is much more pleasant with a good flow of water. Do this hike in winter or on a sunny day after a tradewind storm in summer. As usual with stream hikes, do not attempt the crossings during or right after a heavy rain.

From the top of the waterfall you can continue hiking upstream on a faint trail. It eventually climbs back to the loop trail near the second power-line tower. This extension is, however, unimproved and obscure in places and is strictly for intermediates and above.

Memorize the spot where you first reach the stream for the return trip.

The loop trail receives regular maintenance and is always open. The side ridge and valley trails receive periodic maintenance. The section along the stream overgrows between clearings.

There are some mosquitoes along the stream.

The strawberry guavas usually ripen in August and September.

The initial section of this hike along the loop trail is also part of the 'Aiea Loop and 'Aiea Ridge hikes.

18 Waimano Ridge

Type:	Graded ridge
Length:	15 mi round trip
Elev. Gain:	1,700 ft
Danger:	Low
Suitable for:	Intermediate, Expert
Location:	Leeward Koʻolau Range above Pearl City
Topo Map:	Waipahu, Kāneʻohe
Access:	Open

Trailhead Directions

At Punchbowl St. get on the Lunalilo Fwy (H-1) heading ʻewa (west).

Near Middle St. keep left on Rte 78 west (exit 19B, Moanalua Rd.) to ʻAiea.

By Aloha Stadium bear right to rejoin H-1 to Pearl City.

Leave the freeway at exit 10, marked Pearl City—Waimalu.

At the end of the off ramp, turn right on Moanalua Rd.

At the road end, turn right on Waimano Home Rd.

The road narrows to two lanes.

Enter the grounds of Waimano Training School and Hospital.

Look for the guard station ahead.

Park on the left in a grassy area just before the guard shack and across from three rectangular buildings (map point A).

Route Description

Continue up Waimano Home Rd. on foot.

Bear left off the road by the hiker/hunter check-in kiosk near the guard shack.

Follow the path to the left of and next to a chain-link fence.

Shortly afterward reach a junction (map point B). Keep right, on the Upper Waimano Trail along the fence. (To the left the lower trail leads down into Waimano Valley.)

Parallel the fence and the road, passing several guard rails.

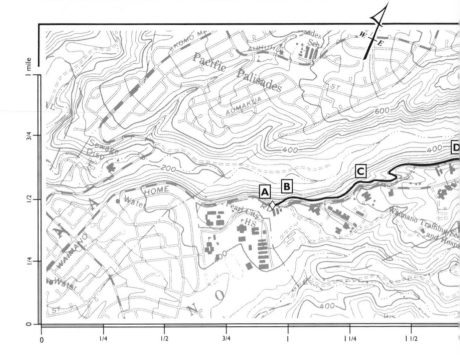

Across from a low, white building turn left and down, still on the upper, ridge trail (map point C).

An abandoned irrigation ditch comes in on the right.

Jump over a narrow concrete spillway.

Bear left into a side gully.

Cross an eroded area with a good view of the Wai'anae Range in the distance.

The ditch reappears on the right and then periodically disappears into short tunnels.

Reach a junction (map point D). Continue straight on the upper trail. (To the left the lower trail leads down to the floor of Waimano Valley.)

Pass several large mango trees.

Descend gradually to a tributary of Waimano Stream.

Just past a dead triple-trunked tree, reach a junction (map point E). Turn left off the wide trail and cross the stream. (The wide trail, which quickly becomes overgrown, climbs out of the valley back to Waimano Training School and Hospital.)

After the crossing, bear right upstream.

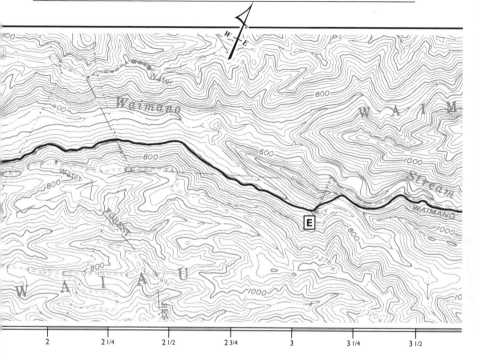

Leave the stream behind and climb the low side ridge on the left with the help of two switchbacks.

Cross over the ridge line at a grassy clearing with a large fallen trunk.

Contour along the left side of the ridge well above Waimano Stream.

Descend to the stream at the ditch intake, which is blocked.

There Waimano Stream forks (map point F). Cross the right fork and take the trail heading upstream along the right side of the left fork.

Climb steadily up the ridge, switchbacking four times (map point G).

Scramble over two small humps in the trail caused by blowdowns.

Reach the top of the ridge in a grove of Australian tea.

Just after climbing a third hump, reach a junction (map point H). Continue straight on the contour trail. (To the right a trail leads down to the right fork of Waimano Stream [crossed earlier] and a dilapidated cabin on the far bank.)

Continue to contour just below the top of the ridge.

Switchback once to gain the ridge line and cross over to its right side (map point I).

Contour in and out of several side gullies.

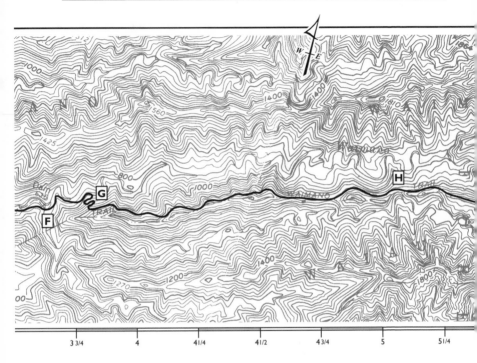

Reach the Koʻolau summit in a saddle just to the right of a large landslide (elev. 2,160 ft) (map point J).

Notes

The Upper Waimano Trail is the best preserved of the graded Koʻolau ridge trails built in the 1930s by the Civilian Conservation Corps. The footing is so good that the miles just seem to fly by. Soon you're in some wild country, and before you know it, you're at the top. On the way back cruise down the mountain.

From the top you can look straight down into Waiheʻe Valley. In the background are Kahaluʻu town and most of Kāneʻohe Bay.

Turn left along the Koʻolau summit to reach the Mānana Trail. The summit section there is frequently clouded over, so it is easy to become disoriented. Up Waimano and down Mānana is a challenging trip for experienced hikers.

The route up Waimano is straightforward except for the two stream crossings. Pay particular attention to the directions at those points.

After the second junction with the lower trail are several narrow spots. There are two cables for assistance.

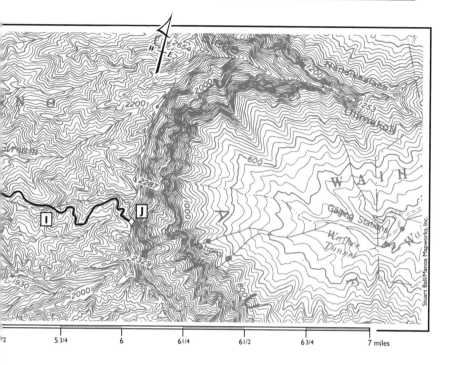

The upper trail receives regular maintenance and is usually open. The middle and upper sections overgrow between clearings.

Don't be put off by the 15-mile length of this hike. The footpath is graded, wide, and very easy on the feet. Try this trail if you have any experience at all. Go as far as you want and then turn around. However, this hike is not recommended for beginners because of the narrow spots mentioned earlier.

The strawberry guavas usually ripen in August and September.

The initial section of the upper trail is the return portion of the Waimano Valley hike.

19 Waimano Valley

Type:	Valley
Length:	2 mi loop
Elev. Gain:	300 ft
Danger:	Low
Suitable for:	Novice
Location:	Leeward Ko'olau Range above Pearl City
Topo Map:	Waipahu
Access:	Open

Trailhead Directions

At Punchbowl St. get on the Lunalilo Fwy (H-1) heading 'ewa (west).

Near Middle St. keep left on Rte 78 west (exit 19B, Moanalua Rd.) to 'Aiea.

By Aloha Stadium bear right to rejoin H-1 to Pearl City.

Leave the freeway at exit 10, marked Pearl City—Waimalu.

At the end of the off ramp, turn right on Moanalua Rd.

At the road end, turn right on Waimano Home Rd.

The road narrows to two lanes.

Enter the grounds of Waimano Training School and Hospital.

Look for the guard station ahead.

Park on the left in a grassy area just before the guard shack and across from three rectangular buildings (map point A).

Route Description

Continue up Waimano Home Rd. on foot.

Bear left off the road by the hiker/hunter check-in kiosk near the guard shack.

Follow the path to the left of and next to a chain-link fence.

Shortly afterward reach a junction (map point B). Bear left on the wide Lower Waimano Trail heading into the valley. (The trail along the fence is the upper trail, which is the return portion of the loop.)

Pass an old wooden sign post on the right.

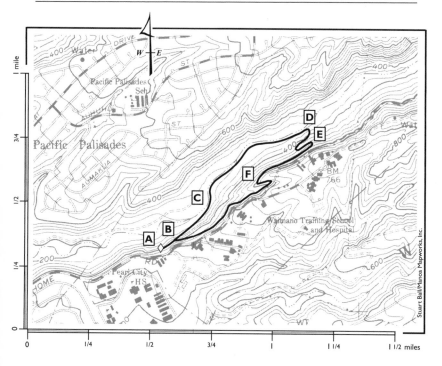

Descend gradually down the side of the ridge on a broad grassy avenue.

The trail narrows through some Christmas berry.

Reach the valley floor (map point C). Keep right, heading upstream.

Pass a hau grove on the left.

The trail comes close to Waimano Stream and parallels it.

Pass a series of hau groves.

The trail begins to climb away from the stream.

Reach a junction marked by two large mango trees in a clearing (map point D). Turn right uphill on a wide trail. (The trail straight ahead continues up the valley.)

The trail narrows.

Work left initially and then straight up the side of the ridge.

Bear left and climb more gradually on two switchbacks.

Halfway up the ridge reach the junction with the Upper Waimano Trail (map point E). Turn sharp right on it. (To the left the trail goes all the way to the Ko'olau summit.)

An abandoned irrigation ditch comes in on the left and parallels the trail. Periodically it disappears into short tunnels.

Climb gradually through eucalyptus.

Bear left across an eroded area (map point F). To the right is a good view of the Wai'anae Range in the distance.

Descend into a side gully. The ditch reappears on the left.

Jump over a narrow concrete spillway.

Turn right along the fence by Waimano Home Rd.

Reach the junction with the lower trail (map point B) and, shortly afterward, the guard shack (map point A).

Notes

This is the perfect hike for a sunny Sunday afternoon. Stroll into Waimano Valley and enjoy the lovely walk by the stream. The climb out is not difficult, but you'll know you've had some exercise!

The trails making up this hike receive regular maintenance and are thus usually clear. The footpath is, for the most part, graded and wide.

The junction in the valley with the trail heading uphill does not jump out at you. Look for the two mango trees and two small stumps. If you miss the junction, go as far as you want up the valley along the stream and then return the same way. The trail up the valley follows the stream for quite a ways.

There are a few mosquitoes in the valley to keep you moving.

The strawberry guavas in the valley and along the upper trail usually ripen in August and September.

The return portion along the upper trail is also part of the Waimano Ridge hike.

20 Waimano Pool

Type:	Valley
Length:	3 mi round trip
Elev. Gain:	600 ft
Danger:	Low
Suitable for:	Novice, Intermediate
Location:	Leeward Koʻolau Range above Pacific Palisades
Topo Map:	Waipahu
Access:	Open

Trailhead Directions

At Punchbowl St. get on the Lunalilo Fwy (H-1) heading ʻewa (west).

Near Middle St. keep left on Rte 78 west (exit 19B, Moanalua Rd.) to ʻAiea.

By Aloha Stadium bear right to rejoin H-1 to Pearl City.

Leave the freeway at exit 10, marked Pearl City—Waimalu.

Turn right on Moanalua Rd. at the end of the off ramp.

As Moanalua Rd. ends, turn right on Waimano Home Rd.

At the third traffic light and just before the road narrows to two lanes, turn left on Komo Mai Dr.

The road descends into Waimano Valley and then climbs the next ridge.

Drive through Pacific Palisades to the end of the road.

Park there on the street just before the turnaround circle (map point A).

Route Description

At the back of the circle walk through an opening in the fence next to the gate.

Proceed up the one-lane paved road.

Reach a water tank at the road end (map point B).

Continue straight, through the eucalyptus, on the Mānana Trail.

Pass a utility tower on the left.

Stroll through a pleasant level section on top of the ridge.

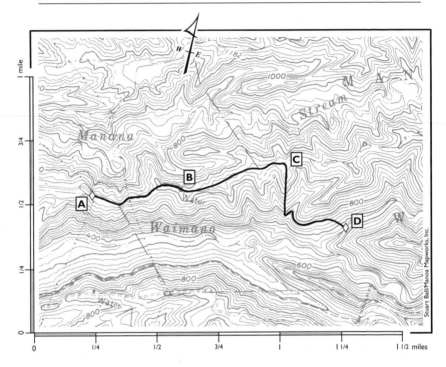

In an open rooty section bear slightly left and down to continue on the main ridge.

At the base of a small hump in the ridge the trail forks (map point C). Bear right and contour around the hump. (The left fork is the continuation of the Mānana Trail. It climbs the hump and goes all the way to the Ko'olau summit.)

Just past the hump keep right on a side ridge leading down to Waimano Valley.

The trail dips and then ascends briefly to a small grassy knoll.

Descend steeply over loose dirt and roots.

Bear left across the face of the side ridge into a small gulch.

Contour out of the gulch on a rough trail.

Descend gradually toward the valley floor.

Contour again. To the right and below, Waimano Stream splits in two.

Bear right and begin the final descent.

Reach the left fork of the stream at the lower pool.

Turn left on a narrow, slippery trail to get to the upper pool at the base of a small waterfall.

The trail continues upstream to the top of the waterfall (map point D).

Notes

Waimano Pool is a popular hike because of its easy access, short length, and two good-sized swimming holes at the end. Do this hike in the rainy season (November–April). After a good rain the stream keeps the pools full of cool, clear water. During summer the stream slows to a trickle and may even dry up.

Although suitable for novices, this hike has several steep, often slippery, stretches. Negotiate them with caution.

The trail receives periodic maintenance and is usually open.

The Mānana hike starts from the same trailhead.

21 Mānana

Type:	Ungraded ridge
Length:	12 mi round trip
Elev. Gain:	1,700 ft
Danger:	Low
Suitable for:	Novice, Intermediate, Expert
Location:	Leeward Koʻolau Range above Pacific Palisades
Topo Map:	Waipahu, Kāneʻohe
Access:	Open

Trailhead Directions

At Punchbowl St. get on the Lunalilo Fwy (H-1) heading ʻewa (west).

Near Middle St. keep left on Rte 78 west (exit 19B, Moanalua Rd.) to ʻAiea.

By Aloha Stadium bear right to rejoin H-1 to Pearl City.

Leave the freeway at exit 10, marked Pearl City—Waimalu.

Turn right on Moanalua Rd. at the end of the off ramp.

As Moanalua Rd. ends, turn right on Waimano Home Rd.

At the third traffic light and just before the road narrows to two lanes, turn left on Komo Mai Dr.

The road descends into Waimano Valley and then climbs the next ridge.

Drive through Pacific Palisades to the end of the road.

Park there on the street just before the turnaround circle (map point A).

Route Description

At the back of the circle walk through an opening in the fence next to the gate.

Proceed up the one-lane paved road.

Reach a water tank at the road end (map point B).

Continue straight, through the eucalyptus, on the Mānana Trail.

Pass a utility tower on the left.

Stroll through a pleasant level section on top of the ridge.

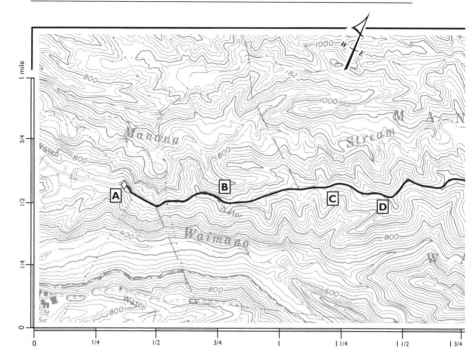

In an open rooty section bear slightly left and down to continue on the main ridge.

At the base of a small hump in the ridge the trail forks (map point C). Bear left and climb the hump. (The right fork, which contours around the hump, leads down to Waimano Valley and is part of the Waimano Pool hike.) This junction is obscure. Look for the hump, which is covered with leaves from the eucalyptus trees.

Descend briefly on an eroded trail.

Climb gradually through a young eucalyptus forest.

After another short descent the trail forks. Bear left and down (map point D).

Break out into the open.

After an initial eroded section, the trail becomes a wide grassy path through the rolling hills. This section is recovering from a fire in the 1970s. The native plants, such as koa, naupaka, and even sandalwood, are coming back nicely.

Descend gradually to a broad saddle.

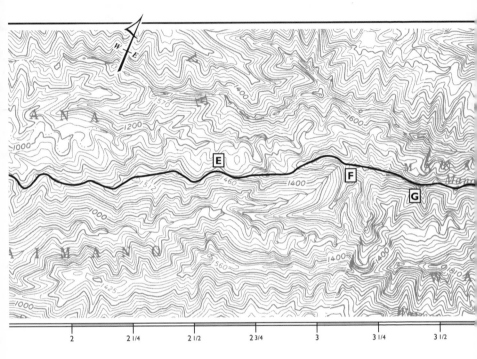

Climb steeply to the first really distinct knob in the ridge (map point E). Just before its top, a large koa trunk has fallen across the trail.

Descend the next dip and ascend steeply to the next hump.

Cross a short level section.

Climb very steeply to another knob, where a long side ridge comes in on the right (map point F).

The trail narrows and becomes rough.

Cross another level section, descend briefly, and then ascend a flat cleared hill used occasionally as a helipad (map point G). There is a view in all directions.

Traverse a series of small but steep knobs in the ridge.

Climb two larger humps and cross a level muddy section.

Ascend steeply to a large hill with a clearing on top (map point H). From there is a commanding view of the ridge as it veers slightly left and then angles back toward the Koʻolau summit.

Climb steadily as the vegetation becomes stunted and the wind picks up.

A long side ridge comes in on the left (map point I).

The main ridge narrows significantly.

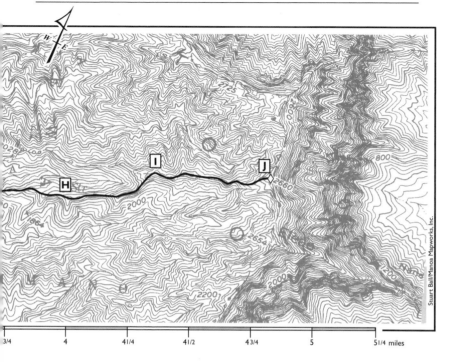

Cross a series of small humps.
The ridge broadens and levels briefly.
Cross a second series of humps.
Pass a waterfall chute down and on the right.
Climb steadily through increasing vegetation.
Reach the Ko'olau summit at a massive knob (elev. 2,660 ft) (map point J).

Notes

Mānana is the best of the ungraded Ko'olau ridge trails. The hike offers over 2 miles of open ridge walking. The wild, windy finish is absolutely wonderful. You feel like you are on top of the world.

On the way to the summit the trail passes through native forest with a good variety of plants. You can spot some of the native birds, such as 'apapane.

The Mānana Trail will appeal to all types of hikers. Novices can stroll through the lower improved section. Intermediate hikers can go as far as the helipad. Experts can head for the summit.

From the top you can see Kāne'ohe Bay and the windward coast to Maka-

pu'u Pt. Ka'alaea Valley is below. Pu'u 'Ōhulehule is on the left, and Olomana, on the right in the distance. Near the shore are Mōli'i and Kahalu'u
fish ponds. On the way up are views of Pearl Harbor and the Wahiawā plain
with the Wai'anae Range in the background.

Turn right along the Ko'olau summit to reach the Upper Waimano Trail.
The summit section here is frequently socked in, so it is easy to become disoriented. Up Mānana and down Waimano is a challenging outing for experienced hikers.

The Mānana Trail receives periodic maintenance. The lower section is well
kept and is always open. The middle section overgrows between clearings.
The wind keeps the upper section open.

The trail is easy to follow for the most part. However, on the initial trail
section remember to keep left on the main ridge. Do not take any of the
side ridges on the right down into Waimano Valley. On the way back from
the summit bear left where the ridge divides.

The Waimano Pool hike starts from the same trailhead.

MILILANI TO WAHIAWĀ

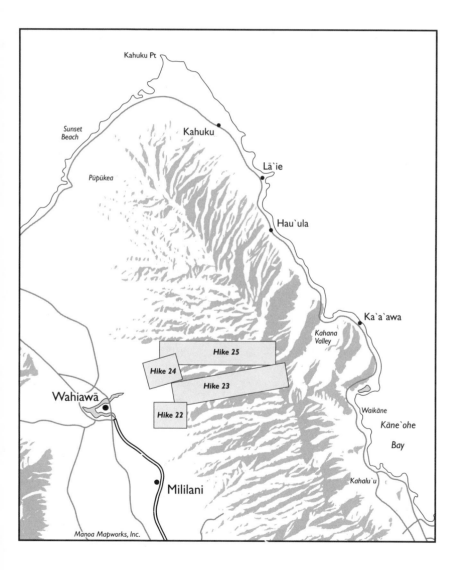

22 Waikakalaua

Type:	Valley
Length:	3 mi loop
Elev. Gain:	200 ft
Danger:	Low
Suitable for:	Novice
Location:	Leeward Ko'olau Range above Mililani
Topo Map:	Waipahu
Access:	Conditional; open to outdoor clubs and organizations with written permission. Write the Directorate of Facilities Engineering, U.S. Army Support Command, Fort Shafter, HI 96858.

Trailhead Directions

At Punchbowl St. get on the Lunalilo Fwy (H-1) heading 'ewa (west).

Near Middle St. keep left on Rte 78 west (exit 19B, Moanalua Rd.) to 'Aiea.

By Aloha Stadium bear right to rejoin H-1 to Pearl City.

Take the H-2 freeway (exit 8A) toward Wahiawā.

Get off H-2 at Wheeler Air Force Base (exit 7, Rte 99 north).

Turn left at the top of the off ramp.

At the road end, turn right on Kamehameha Hwy (Rte 99 north).

At the first traffic light and across from the Wheeler AFB gate, turn right on a paved military road.

Go underneath the freeway.

Check in with the guard at the sentry box on the left. Reset your trip odometer.

Enter the East Range, a training area used by the Army at Schofield Barracks.

Pass the NCO Academy on the left (1.2 mi).

Reach a three-way fork (1.6 mi). Bear right on the middle fork, which is paved, but narrower. (The left fork leads down to the South Fork of

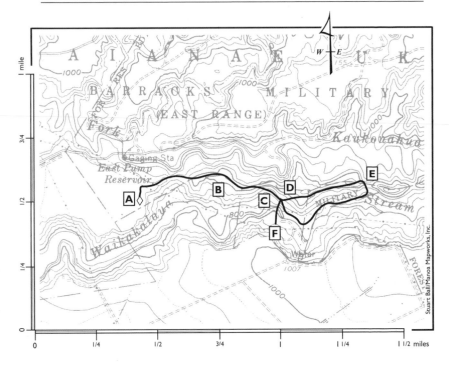

Kaukonahua Stream and the start of the Schofield-Waikāne hike. The right fork is a rough dirt road.)

At the road end, turn left on another narrow paved road (1.9 mi).

Pass a large water tank on the right.

The road splits (2.0 mi). Take the left fork on a dirt road.

Right after the fork, park under the eucalyptus trees on the left (map point A).

Route Description

Continue along the dirt road on foot.

Pass two sets of utility poles on the right.

Descend briefly and then begin climbing along the broad ridge.

An overgrown dirt road comes in on the right. Continue straight on the main road.

The road forks (map point B). Turn right and down.

Descend gradually along the side of Waikakalaua Gulch.

Pass some more utility poles on the right.

As the bottom of the gulch approaches, another dirt road comes in on the right. Keep left upstream. (The road to the right heads downstream.)

As the road levels off momentarily, reach an obscure junction with a trail (map point C). For now, continue straight on the road. (The trail leads down to the swimming hole.) The junction is close to an albizia tree and a semipermanent mud hole in the road.

Look for the dull red portal of a tunnel on the left (map point D).

Enter the tunnel through wide doors.

Pass several side tunnels on the left and right. Keep to the main corridor.

Just before it ends, the tunnel curves right.

Emerge into the sunlight and turn right on a dirt road (map point E). Pass a side entrance to the tunnel on the right.

Reach the tunnel portal again, now on the right (map point D). This completes the short loop section of the hike.

Retrace your steps to the junction with the swimming hole trail. Turn left and down on it.

Just past an eroded section turn left, heading upstream.

Reach Waikakalaua Stream at a good-sized swimming hole (map point F).

Retrace your steps up the trail, turn left on the road, and walk back to your car (map point A).

Notes

Waikakalaua has two main attractions: a beautiful swimming hole and a ¼-mile walk underground through a cavernous tunnel. During World War II the tunnel was used as an underground assembly point for aircraft shipped in pieces from the mainland.

Bring a flashlight for the tunnel.

There are some mosquitoes around the pool.

The road and trail sections receive periodic maintenance and are usually open.

The Schofield-Waikāne hike has the same road access up to the three-way fork.

23 Schofield-Waikāne

Type:	Graded ridge
Length:	12 mi round trip
Elev. Gain:	1,000 ft
Danger:	Low
Suitable for:	Novice, Intermediate, Expert
Location:	Leeward Koʻolau Range above Wahiawā
Topo Map:	Waipahu, Hauʻula
Access:	Conditional; open to individuals and organized groups with written permission. Write the Directorate of Facilities Engineering, U.S. Army Support Command, Fort Shafter, HI 96858.

Trailhead Directions

At Punchbowl St. get on the Lunalilo Fwy (H-1) heading ʻewa (west).

Near Middle St. keep left on Rte 78 west (exit 19B, Moanalua Rd.) to ʻAiea.

By Aloha Stadium bear right to rejoin H-1 to Pearl City.

Take the H-2 freeway (exit 8A) toward Wahiawā.

Get off H-2 at Wheeler Air Force Base (exit 7, Rte 99 north).

Turn left at the top of the off ramp.

At the road end turn right on Kamehameha Hwy (Rte 99 north).

At the first traffic light and across from the Wheeler AFB gate, turn right on a paved military road.

Go underneath the freeway.

Check in with the guard at the sentry box on the left.

Enter the East Range, a training area used by the Army at Schofield Barracks.

Pass the NCO Academy on the left.

Reach a three-way fork. Bear left and down on a gravel/dirt road. (The middle fork leads to the start of the Waikakalaua hike. The right fork is a rough dirt road.)

Cross the South Fork of Kaukonahua Stream on a one-lane bridge.

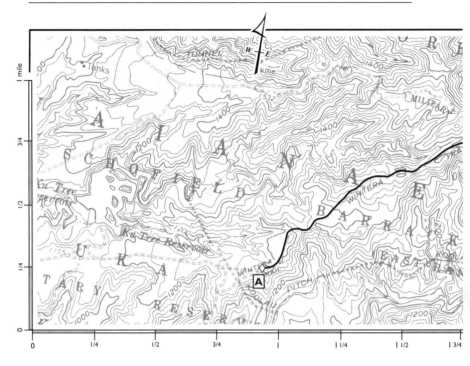

Keep to the main dirt road. Each fork mentioned below is the more traveled way.

Take the left fork heading uphill. The road narrows.

Take the right fork in a flat, well-used area.

Pass several training sites on both sides of the road.

Take the left fork and climb gradually through an open grassy area.

Park in a dirt lot on the right just before reaching the forest (map point A). The lot is backed by a grove of tall eucalyptus trees. Just beyond the lot is a rain gauge in a small enclosure on the left side of the road.

Route Description

Continue along the dirt road on foot.

The road deteriorates during a series of ups and downs.

Break out into the open along the top of the ridge.

As the road turns sharp left and down, heading back toward Wahiawā, bear right on the Schofield-Waikāne Trail (map point B). It starts just to the right of a small hump in the ridge.

Descend briefly on a switchback.

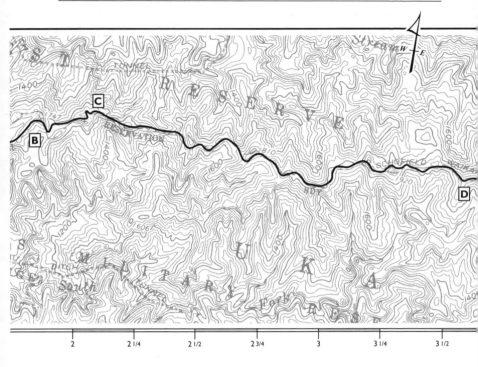

Jump over a deep, but narrow, cut in the ridge.

Contour on the left and then on the right side of the ridge.

Reach a junction (map point C). Take the right fork heading up the ridge. (The left fork leads down to the North Fork of Kaukonahua Stream.)

Contour along the right side of the ridge for a long stretch (and I mean long). Occasionally the trail shifts to the actual ridge line or to its left side.

Cross a relatively level section on top of the ridge (map point D). The vegetation is lower there because of the wind.

Climb steadily now following the crest of the ridge. The trail contours to the right twice and to the left once to skirt humps in the ridge.

Begin the last contour section around the right side of a large peak along the summit ridge (map point E).

Step on some metal roofing, all that's left of an old shelter.

On the right just before the top pass a small open area with good views of the Wai'anae Range.

Reach the Ko'olau summit (elev. 2,360 ft) (map point F) and the junction with the Ko'olau Summit Trail.

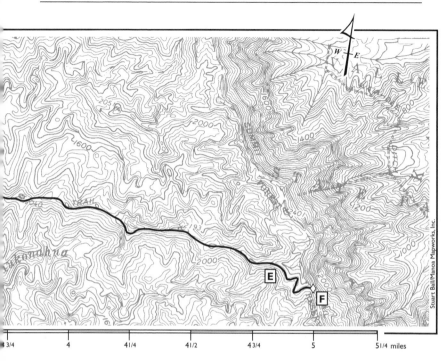

Notes

Schofield-Waikāne is another long, rugged ridge hike in the central Koʻolau Range. It crosses country so wild it's hard to believe you're on populous Oʻahu. The last third of the hike is along an open ridge with views in all directions. The trail ends at a scenic overlook of the windward coast.

From the top you can see four undeveloped valleys. From left to right they are Kahana, Kaʻaʻawa, Hakipuʻu, and Waikāne. Puʻu ʻŌhulehule is the peak dead ahead.

The Schofield-Waikāne Trail receives sporadic maintenance. Much of it goes through uluhe ferns, which overgrow quickly between clearings. As a result, the trail is overgrown and little used. The approach road and the trail to the stream are open.

Although basically graded, the trail has some uneven and narrow spots because of erosion and slippage through the years. The vegetation on the high side tends to force you off the trail. Expect to fall down and get muddy and wet.

For a much easier hike take the side trail to the left down to the North

Fork of Kaukonahua Stream. There are good swimming holes both up and down stream.

An alternate access is available from the end of California Ave. in Wahiawā. See the trailhead directions for the Wahiawā Hills hike. Walk around the back of the large water tanks and turn left on the dirt road. Reach the start of the Schofield-Waikāne Trail where the road turns sharp right and heads back toward Wheeler AFB. This route adds another 2 miles to the hike. Permission is required from the Army.

The Koʻolau Summit Trail is a graded footpath that winds along the crest of the Koʻolau Range from the end of Pūpūkea Rd. to the end of the Kīpapa Ridge Trail. At the end of Schofield-Waikāne turn left to reach the Poamoho Cabin and Poamoho Ridge Trail and points north. The Summit Trail is for experienced hikers only because it is overgrown, muddy, and sometimes narrow and obscure.

The Schofield-Waikāne Trail is also known as the Wahiawā Trail.

24 Wahiawā Hills

Type:	Foothill
Length:	5 mi loop
Elev. Gain:	600 ft
Danger:	Low
Suitable for:	Intermediate
Location:	Leeward Koʻolau Range above Wahiawā
Topo Map:	Hauʻula
Access:	Conditional; open to individuals and organized groups with written permission. Write the Directorate of Facilities Engineering, U.S. Army Support Command, Fort Shafter, HI 96858.

Trailhead Directions

At Punchbowl St. get on the Lunalilo Fwy (H-1) heading ʻewa (west).

Near Middle St. keep left on Rte 78 west (exit 19B, Moanalua Rd.) to ʻAiea.

By Aloha Stadium bear right to rejoin H-1 to Pearl City.

Take the H-2 freeway (exit 8A) toward Wahiawā.

Get off H-2 at Wahiawā (exit 8, Rte 80 north).

At the end of the off ramp merge into Kamehameha Hwy.

Cross Wilson Bridge and enter Wahiawā town.

Just past Burger King turn right on California Ave.

The road narrows to two lanes.

Pass Leilehua High School on the right.

The road jogs right and then left.

Drive to the end of California Ave. near two large, green water tanks.

Park there on the street (map point A).

Route Description

Take the trail starting at the end of the pavement. Initially, it parallels the fence surrounding the water tanks.

97

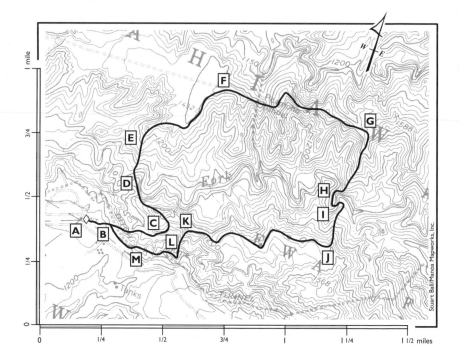

Angle left through the eucalyptus toward the edge of a ridge. The way is confusing because the understory is open, and there are many side trails.

Follow the path along the edge of the ridge.

Reach an obscure junction (map point B). Turn left and descend steeply down a side ridge. (The trail to the right is the return portion of the loop.)

As the ridge levels off, bear left off of it on a graded trail.

Descend gradually into a gully.

Just below a tiny waterfall turn left and cross a stream (map point C).

Climb the opposite bank and turn right, heading upstream.

Switchback once, leaving the stream behind.

Bear right and climb straight up the ridge.

Gain the ridge line and turn left.

Descend gradually along the ridge.

Cross a narrow neck with the North Fork of Kaukonahua Stream on the right and the smaller stream just crossed on the left.

After climbing briefly, the ridge levels off. Turn right down a side ridge.

Two-thirds of the way down bear left off the side ridge and descend to Kaukonahua Stream.

Head downstream briefly and then turn right to cross the stream.

The ford is wide and shallow with overhanging trees on the far side (map point D).

Scramble up the steep bank and then ascend gradually through the forest.

Climb steeply up a side ridge covered with uluhe ferns. There is a good view of the Wai'anae Range to the left.

Near a grove of koa trees gain the main ridge line (map point E) and turn right along it.

Join an overgrown dirt road.

Reach a junction with another dirt road. Cross it onto a trail.

Bear left across a flat area with eucalyptus.

Cross a line of rusty metal stakes.

Stroll through the forest on a broad ridge. Keep to the right along its edge.

Break out into the open through a stretch of uluhe ferns.

Reach another junction with the previous dirt road (map point F). Turn right on it. (The trail across the road leads down to Poamoho Stream.)

After a brief descent the road ends. Continue along the ridge on a trail.

A side ridge comes in on the left. Keep right on the main ridge.

Work around the base of a huge uprooted tree across the trail.

Another side ridge comes in on the right. Keep left.

In a grove of paperbark trees bear left to bypass a hump in the ridge.

Regain the ridge line.

Shortly afterward the ridge levels and then climbs slightly to a breezy lookout (map point G). From there is a good view mauka toward the Ko'olau summit.

At the lookout turn right down a side ridge.

The ridge splits into two fingers. Take the right one.

Descend steeply toward the North Fork of Kaukonahua Stream.

Cross a narrow neck. The stream takes a sharp bend at the end of the ridge and so is visible on both sides.

Shortly afterward reach a junction. Turn right and descend to a long, deep, and inviting pool (map point H).

When you've had enough swimming and sunning, retrace your steps to the junction and turn right to continue along the finger ridge.

Bear left around the tip of the finger and descend to the stream.

Ford it just below another pool, somewhat smaller than the first (map point I).

Bear right up a side ridge.

Climb steeply through uluhe ferns.

In a clearing reach the top of the main ridge (map point J) and turn right along it.

Follow the edge of the broad ridge through uluhe.

A side ridge comes in on the right. Keep left.

Enter a eucalyptus forest with uluhe as a ground cover. The ridge is a series of ups and downs.

The ridge narrows and then flattens.

Angle left and down, off the ridge crest, through a paperbark grove (map point K).

Bear left down a side ridge.

Descend very steeply to a small stream (map point L).

Cross it and turn left upstream.

Turn sharp right up a side ridge.

As the ridge broadens, work to its right side.

Bear right along the flank of the ridge.

Reach an abandoned irrigation ditch and turn right alongside it.

As the ditch goes into a tunnel, bear right around a bulge in the ridge.

The ditch reappears on the left.

At a spillway cross the ditch (map point M).

Bear left and switchback once.

Climb gradually up the side of the ridge.

Pass a metal post on the right.

Turn right just before reaching a dirt road in the East Range, an Army training area.

Cross an overgrown dirt road.

Keep right along the edge of the ridge.

Reach the original junction (map point B).

Angle left through the eucalyptus forest toward the water tanks and the access to California Ave. (map point A).

Notes

The Wahiawā Hills hike is a true test of my ability to write clear directions and your ability to follow them. The hike is a loop with many twists and turns and ups and downs. You cross two streams twice and climb and descend three ridges. The reward for all this meandering is a delightful swimming hole in Kaukonahua Stream.

That stream is the longest in the State of Hawaii. It is well known for its clear water and deep pools. This hike passes two of the best.

To get to the pools sooner, start the loop in reverse. After your swim, continue on the loop or come back the same way.

Do not attempt to cross Kaukonahua Stream during or right after a heavy rain. If you are caught on the far side and the water rises significantly, wait until the stream goes down. Notice the debris on the shrubs and trees lining the stream. That's how high the stream gets during a bad storm!

There are some mosquitoes along the streams.

The trails on this hike receive periodic maintenance. The uluhe ferns on the side ridges and along the main ridge on the return overgrow quickly between clearings. The rest of the hike is usually open.

The end of California Ave. is also the alternate access for the Schofield-Waikāne hike.

25 Poamoho Ridge

Type:	Graded ridge
Length:	12 mi round trip (from forest boundary)
Elev. Gain:	1,000 ft
Danger:	Low
Suitable for:	Novice, Intermediate, Expert
Location:	Leeward Koʻolau Range above Helemano
Topo Map:	Hauʻula
Access:	Conditional; open to individuals and organized groups with written permission. Contact Castle & Cooke Land Development Co., P.O. Box 2900, Honolulu, HI 96802; Waialua Sugar Co. (phone 637–3521); and the Directorate of Facilities Engineering, U.S. Army Support Command, Fort Shafter, HI 96858.

Trailhead Directions

At Punchbowl St. get on the Lunalilo Fwy (H-1) heading ʻewa (west).

Near Middle St. keep left on Rte 78 west (exit 19B, Moanalua Rd.) to ʻAiea.

By Aloha Stadium bear right to rejoin H-1 to Pearl City.

Take the H-2 freeway (exit 8A) to Wahiawā.

As the freeway ends, continue on Rte 99 north (Wilikina Dr.) bypassing Wahiawā.

Pass Schofield Barracks on the left.

The road narrows to two lanes, dips, and then forks. Take the right fork to Haleʻiwa (Kamananui Rd., but still Rte 99 north).

At the road end turn left on Kamehameha Hwy.

Pass the Dole Pavilion and Helemano Plantation on the right.

Just past a bus stop, turn right on the paved road that borders the plantation. Reset your trip odometer.

Pass a water tank on the left (0.1 mi).

Before the pavement ends, bear slightly left on a well-traveled dirt road (0.2 mi).

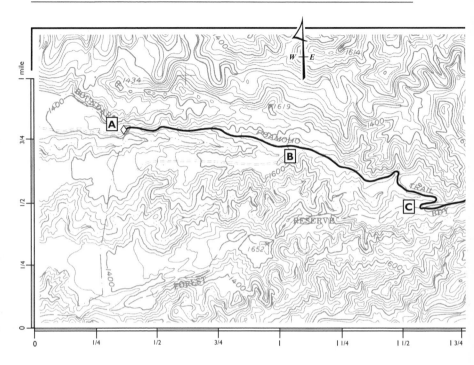

The road parallels a line of utility poles through the pineapple fields.

At a small concrete building, turn right (1.1 mi) and circle around Hele-mano Military Reservation. There is a grass strip on the left.

In back of the reservation, turn right (1.8 mi), leaving the grass strip behind.

The road forks (2.1 mi). Bear left.

Descend briefly through a narrow swath of forest (2.6 mi).

Climb gradually to the top of the last pineapple field.

Reach the forest reserve boundary (3.85 mi) (map point A) and park there along the road.

If the road is dry and the weather looks good, continue through the forest to an open area on the right (4.6 mi) (map point B) and park there.

Route Description

Continue along the dirt road on foot.

After passing a second open area on the right, the road descends briefly.

Switchback twice to gain altitude gradually (map point C).

Reach the road end and the start of the Poamoho Ridge Trail (map point D).

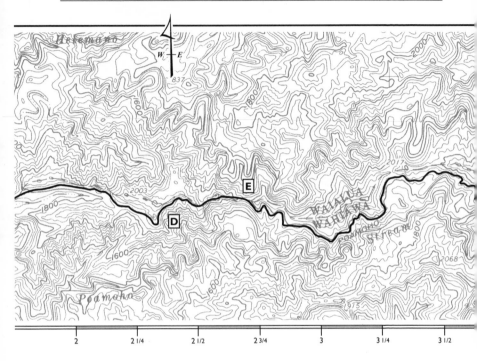

The trail contours briefly on the right side of the ridge and then crosses over to the left.

Pass a good view point on the right.

Switch to the right side of the ridge (map point E) and contour for a long stretch.

As the ridge narrows, the trail follows the crest briefly and then continues on the left side of the ridge (map point F).

Gain the ridge line briefly and then resume contouring on the left side.

Work up a side gulch above a small stream (map point G).

Descend to the stream and cross it.

Turn left back downstream.

Cross over to the right side of the ridge. The stream is now on the right.

Ascend gradually, leaving the stream behind.

Bear right to cross a windy grassy area.

Reach the junction with the Koʻolau Summit Trail at the stone memorial to Geraldine Cline.

Keep the memorial on the left and ascend a small grassy hump to reach the Koʻolau summit (elev. 2,520 ft) (map point H).

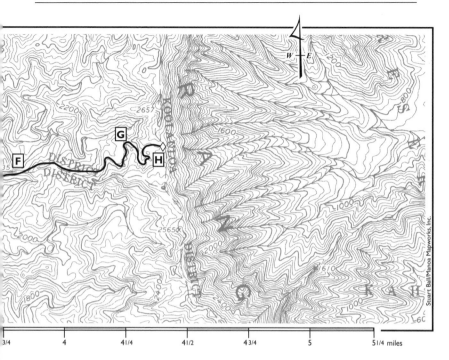

Notes

The leeward Ko'olau ridge hikes in central O'ahu are long and rugged. Poamoho is no exception although the road at the beginning does make the hike easier. The trail passes through some truly wild country and ends at a windy overlook with one of the best views on the island. The variety of native plants on the upper section is especially good. You can also see native birds, such as 'apapane and 'amakihi.

From the top you can look down on two broad undeveloped valleys, Punalu'u and Kahana. The sharp peak on the right is Pu'u 'Ōhulehule. In front of it and partially hidden is Ka'a'awa Valley.

The condition of the dirt road from the forest reserve boundary to the trailhead varies from year to year. The conservative approach is to park your car at the reserve boundary. Starting from there, the hike is the full 12 miles. If the road and weather conditions are good, drive another mile to the open area on the right. The hike then becomes 10 miles. Continue farther along the road only if you have four-wheel drive.

The Poamoho Ridge Trail receives periodic maintenance. The lower and middle sections overgrow quickly between clearings. The upper section is usually open.

The trail is basically graded but has some uneven and narrow spots because of erosion and slippage through the years. Watch your footing constantly. Expect to fall down and get muddy and wet. Novice and intermediate hikers can go as far as they like and then turn around.

Poamoho makes a good camping trip. There is a sheltered campsite just before crossing the small stream. You can also stay at the Poamoho Cabin, which is a half mile along the Koʻolau Summit Trail to the right. The cabin has a water tank and a pit toilet. Reserve the cabin with the Forestry and Wildlife Division, Department of Land and Natural Resources, Room 325, 1151 Punchbowl St. (phone 587–0166).

The Koʻolau Summit Trail is a graded footpath that winds along the crest of the Koʻolau Range from the end of Pūpūkea Rd. to the end of the Kīpapa Ridge Trail. At the Cline memorial junction turn right to get to the Schofield-Waikāne Trail. Turn left to reach Kawailoa Ridge and Lāʻie Trails. The mileage to each trail junction is listed on the Cline memorial. The Koʻolau Summit Trail is for experienced hikers only because it is overgrown, muddy, and sometimes narrow and obscure.

Geraldine Cline was a beloved member of the Hawaiian Trail and Mountain Club. She died tragically in an automobile accident.

HALEʻIWA TO PŪPŪKEA

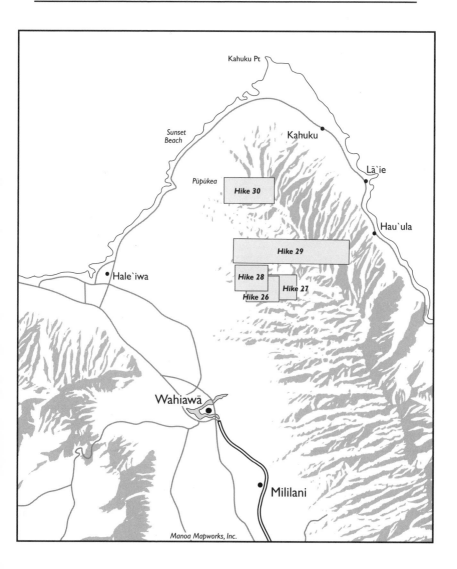

Kahuku Pt

Sunset
Beach

Kahuku

Lāʻie

Pūpūkea

Hike 30

Hauʻula

Hike 29

Hike 28

Hike 27

Hike 26

• Haleʻiwa

Wahiawā

Mililani

Manoa Mapworks, Inc.

26 'Ōpae'ula

Type:	Valley
Length:	2 mi round trip
Elev. Gain:	200 ft
Danger:	Low
Suitable for:	Novice
Location:	Leeward Ko'olau Range above Hale'iwa
Topo Map:	Hau'ula
Access:	Conditional; open only to outdoor clubs and organizations with permission. Contact Waialua Sugar Co. (phone 637–3521) and the Directorate of Facilities Engineering, U.S. Army Support Command, Fort Shafter, HI 96858.

Trailhead Directions

At Punchbowl St. get on the Lunalilo Fwy (H-1) heading 'ewa (west).

Near Middle St. keep left on Rte 78 west (exit 19B, Moanalua Rd.) to 'Aiea.

By Aloha Stadium bear right to rejoin H-1 to Pearl City.

Take the H-2 freeway (exit 8A) to Wahiawā.

As the freeway ends, continue on Rte 99 north (Wilikina Dr.) bypassing Wahiawā.

Pass Schofield Barracks on the left.

The road narrows to two lanes, dips, and then forks. Take the right fork to Hale'iwa (Kamananui Rd., but still Rte 99 north).

At the road end turn left on Kamehameha Hwy.

Pass Dole Plantation on the right.

In Weed Circle, bear right into Hale'iwa town (still Kamehameha Hwy, but now Rte 83).

Just past Lili'uokalani Protestant Church with its brown-and-white steeple, turn right on Emerson Rd.

As the pavement ends, turn sharp right on a paved cane haul road.

Take the first left on paved 'Ōpae'ula Rd.

Reach a locked gate and reset your trip odometer.

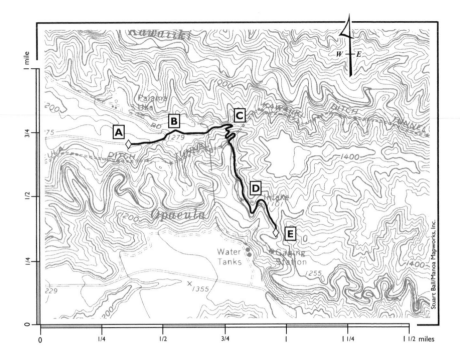

Ascend gradually through the sugarcane fields.

The road forks (1.5 mi). Keep right on the main road paralleling 'Ōpae'ula Gulch.

The road narrows and then becomes dirt.

'Ōpae'ula Rd. ends at a reservoir (5.2 mi). Continue straight on Pa'ala'a Uka Pūpūkea Rd., used by the military.

Pass 'Ōpae'ula Lodge on the right in a grove of eucalyptus trees (5.4 mi).

The road forks (6.2 mi). Keep right, on the military road, which is narrower but more heavily used.

Reach the top of the last cane field (6.6 mi). Park near two koa trees just before the road descends and turns sharp left (map point A). Leave plenty of room for plantation and military vehicles to get by.

Route Description

Continue along the military road on foot.

It descends briefly and then turns sharp left. At the turn bear right on a rough dirt road (map point B).

At the road end continue straight on a trail along the ridge line.

Descend briefly through a grove of eucalyptus trees.
As the trail starts to climb, reach a junction (map point C). Turn right and down, into 'Ōpae'ula Gulch. (The trail straight ahead leads into Kawai Iki Gulch.)
Descend on a series of switchbacks through a stand of strawberry guava.
Reach the junction of the 'Ōpae'ula and Kawai Iki ditches.
Cross the 'Ōpae'ula ditch on a plank and turn left, heading upstream.
Contour above 'Ōpae'ula Stream. The ditch takes a more direct route, tunneling through the cliffs, rather than going around them as the trail does.
Cross a ditch overflow channel on a short plank.
Pass a concrete dam and the ditch intake on the right (map point D).
Descend to the stream and cross it by some large smooth rocks.
Cross the stream two more times and then enter a bamboo grove.
Reach a small clearing with a swimming hole (map point E).

Notes

'Ōpae'ula is a short, pleasant stream hike. The small pool at the end is a welcome sight on a hot summer day. If you are feeling energetic, it is possible to explore farther upstream.

If the plank across 'Ōpae'ula ditch is gone, turn right and down, along the ditch and walk underneath it through a short tunnel.

To avoid the three stream crossings, walk across the top of the dam. Climb steeply up the opposite bank, heading upstream. Turn left and descend to the swimming hole past a dilapidated outhouse and equipment shed.

Do not attempt the stream or dam crossings during or right after a heavy rain.

The trail receives periodic maintenance. It overgrows slowly between clearings.

The strawberry guavas usually ripen in late July and August.

There are a few mosquitoes down by the stream.

The initial section along the dirt road and the ridge is also part of the Kawai Iki hike. The Kawainui hike has the same road access.

The 'Ōpae'ula and Kawai Iki ditches empty into the reservoir you passed on the drive up. The Waialua Sugar Co. uses the water to irrigate its cane fields.

The Pa'ala'a Uka Pūpūkea Rd. is a military thoroughfare that winds through the foothills of the leeward Ko'olau Range. It starts at Helemano Military Reservation near the Poamoho Ridge hike and finishes by the end of Pūpūkea Rd. near the Kaunala hike.

27 Kawai Iki

Type:	Valley
Length:	5 mi round trip
Elev. Gain:	200 ft
Danger:	Low
Suitable for:	Novice
Location:	Leeward Ko'olau Range above Hale'iwa
Topo Map:	Hau'ula
Access:	Conditional; open only to outdoor clubs and organizations with permission. Contact Waialua Sugar Co. (phone 637–3521) and the Directorate of Facilities Engineering, U.S. Army Support Command, Fort Shafter, HI 96858.

Trailhead Directions

At Punchbowl St. get on the Lunalilo Fwy (H-1) heading 'ewa (west).

Near Middle St. keep left on Rte 78 west (exit 19B, Moanalua Rd.) to 'Aiea.

By Aloha Stadium bear right to rejoin H-1 to Pearl City.

Take the H-2 freeway (exit 8A) to Wahiawā.

As the freeway ends, continue on Rte 99 north (Wilikina Dr.) bypassing Wahiawā.

Pass Schofield Barracks on the left.

The road narrows to two lanes, dips, and then forks. Take the right fork to Hale'iwa (Kamananui Rd., but still Rte 99 north).

At the road end, turn left on Kamehameha Hwy.

Pass Dole Plantation on the right.

In Weed Circle, bear right into Hale'iwa town (still Kamehameha Hwy, but now Rte 83).

Just past Lili'uokalani Protestant Church with its brown-and-white steeple, turn right on Emerson Rd.

As the pavement ends, turn sharp right on a paved cane haul road.

Take the first left on paved 'Ōpae'ula Rd.

Reach a locked gate and reset your trip odometer.

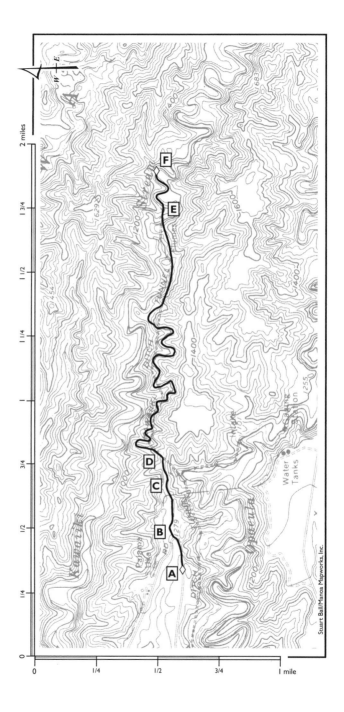

Ascend gradually through the sugarcane fields.

The road forks (1.5 mi). Keep right on the main road paralleling 'Ōpae'ula Gulch.

The road narrows and then becomes dirt.

'Ōpae'ula Rd. ends at a reservoir (5.2 mi). Continue straight on Pa'ala'a Uka Pūpūkea Rd., used by the military.

Pass 'Ōpae'ula Lodge on the right in a grove of eucalyptus trees (5.4 mi).

The road forks (6.2 mi). Keep right, on the military road, which is narrower but more heavily used.

Reach the top of the last cane field (6.6 mi). Park near two koa trees just before the road descends and turns sharp left (map point A). Leave plenty of room for plantation and military vehicles to get by.

Route Description

Continue along the military road on foot.

It descends briefly and then turns sharp left. At the turn bear right on a rough dirt road (map point B).

At the road end continue straight on a trail along the ridge line.

Descend briefly through a grove of eucalyptus trees.

As the trail starts to climb, reach a junction (map point C). Continue straight along the ridge top. (The trail to the right leads down into 'Ōpae'ula Gulch.)

Go to the right of a small hump in the ridge.

Just before a second, smaller hump reach another junction (map point D). Turn left and down, into Kawai Iki Gulch.

Descend gradually on a series of switchbacks.

About halfway down begin contouring along the side of the gulch. The Kawai Iki ditch comes into view several times as the trail works into the side ravines.

Parallel the ditch on its left.

Cross a small, but deep, ravine. Use the steep trail on the left. The boardwalk on the ditch trestle is too rickety.

Continue to parallel the ditch on its left.

Descend to Kawai Iki Stream through a dense grove of strawberry guava.

Cross the stream. Take the steep trail on the right or walk in the ditch across the trestle.

Contour briefly above the stream.

Reach a dam, the ditch intake, and the end of the improved trail (map point E).

Continue upstream on an obscure trail. Stay on the left bank initially and then cross to the right just before a small pool.

Cross two more times to avoid the sheer outer banks of the stream as it turns first left and then right.

After the third crossing reach two swimming holes separated by a large rock (map point F).

Notes

The Kawai Iki hike is a relaxing stroll in a small lovely valley. The ditch with its trestles adds to the interest and enjoyment. The pools at the end are cool and inviting.

You can explore farther upstream. There are bigger and better pools just around the next bend, or so I'm told!

Do not attempt the stream crossings during or right after a heavy rain.

The trail receives periodic maintenance. It overgrows quickly between clearings.

The strawberry guavas usually ripen in late July and August.

There are a few mosquitoes down by the stream.

The initial section along the dirt road and the ridge is also part of the 'Ōpae'ula hike. The Kawainui hike has the same road access.

The Kawai Iki ditch empties into the reservoir you passed on the drive up. The Waialua Sugar Co. uses the water to irrigate its cane fields.

The Pa'ala'a Uka Pūpūkea Rd. is a military thoroughfare that winds through the foothills of the leeward Ko'olau Range. It starts at Helemano Military Reservation near the Poamoho Ridge hike and finishes by the end of Pūpūkea Rd. near the Kaunala hike.

28 Kawainui

Type:	Valley
Length:	6 mi round trip
Elev. Gain:	600 ft
Danger:	Low
Suitable for:	Novice, Intermediate
Location:	Leeward Koʻolau Range above Haleʻiwa
Topo Map:	Hauʻula
Access:	Conditional; open only to outdoor clubs and organizations with permission. Contact Waialua Sugar Co. (phone 637-3521) and the Directorate of Facilities Engineering, U.S. Army Support Command, Fort Shafter, HI 96858.

Trailhead Directions

At Punchbowl St. get on the Lunalilo Fwy (H-1) heading ʻewa (west).

Near Middle St. keep left on Rte 78 west (exit 19B, Moanalua Rd.) to ʻAiea.

By Aloha Stadium bear right to rejoin H-1 to Pearl City.

Take the H-2 freeway (exit 8A) to Wahiawā.

As the freeway ends, continue on Rte 99 north (Wilikina Dr.) bypassing Wahiawā.

Pass Schofield Barracks on the left.

The road narrows to two lanes, dips, and then forks. Take the right fork to Haleʻiwa (Kamananui Rd., but still Rte 99 north).

At the road end turn left on Kamehameha Hwy.

Pass Dole Plantation on the right.

In Weed Circle, bear right into Haleʻiwa town (still Kamehameha Hwy, but now Rte 83).

Just past Liliʻuokalani Protestant Church with its brown-and-white steeple, turn right on Emerson Rd.

As the pavement ends, turn sharp right on a paved cane haul road.

Take the first left on paved ʻŌpaeʻula Rd.

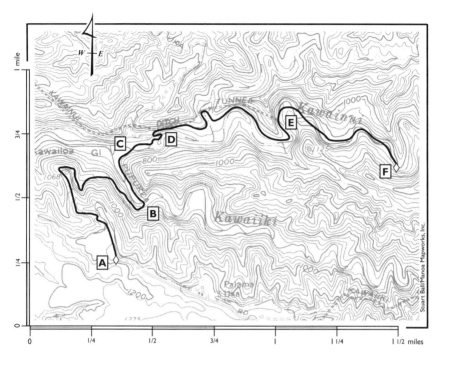

Reach a locked gate and reset your trip odometer.

Ascend gradually through the sugarcane fields.

The road forks (1.5 mi). Keep right on the main road paralleling 'Ōpae'ula Gulch.

The road narrows and then becomes dirt.

'Ōpae'ula Rd. ends at a reservoir (5.2 mi). Continue straight on Pa'ala'a Uka Pūpūkea Rd., used by the military.

Pass 'Ōpae'ula Lodge on the right in a grove of eucalyptus trees (5.4 mi).

The road forks (6.2 mi). Keep right, on the military road, which is narrower but more heavily used.

At the top of the cane fields descend briefly into a small gulch and turn sharp left (6.8 mi).

Climb out of the gulch and pass Pālama Uka Camp on the right (7.0 mi).

Just before the road begins to descend steeply, park in a dirt lot on the left (7.4 mi) (map point A).

Route Description

Continue down the military road on foot.

Descend the side of the ridge into Kawai Iki Gulch.

Cross Kawai Iki Stream on a concrete culvert (map point B).

Bear left, heading downstream.

Leaving the stream behind, bear right into Kawainui Gulch.

Cross Kawainui Stream on a bridge (map point C).

Bear right, heading upstream.

As the road turns sharp left to leave the gulch, bear right on a trail (map point D).

Climb a short, steep section and then turn right through some Christmas berry.

Climb again, this time on two switchbacks. On the right is a short access tunnel to the Kawainui ditch.

Contour along the side of the gulch well above the stream.

Cross a small side stream.

Descend to Kawainui Stream (map point E). The improved trail ends here at a stone dam. The ditch intake is just upstream on the left.

Cross the stream on the dam and bear left on an ungraded trail.

Cross the stream 10 more times. Highlights are as follows: Between 3 and 4: a short, steep descent and a hau grove. Just after 4: a large pool on the left. Between 5 and 6: a large hau grove. After 7: walk in the dry stream bed. Just after 9: a small, round pool.

Reach a lovely pool ringed with kukui trees (map point F).

Notes

The circular pool at the end is the most beautiful one on the island. It is also one of the largest and is great for swimming. With such an attraction this hike is very popular with local clubs for day trips and camping.

Most people stop at the pool; however, further exploration of the gulch is possible. Swim across the pool and continue upstream.

Do not attempt the stream crossings during or right after a heavy rain.

The trail receives periodic maintenance. It overgrows slowly between clearings.

There are a few mosquitoes down by the stream.

The strawberry guavas ripen in August and September, and the mountain apples, in July and early August.

Nearby hikes with the same road access are Kawai Iki and ʻŌpaeʻula.

The Paʻalaʻa Uka Pūpūkea Rd. is a military thoroughfare that winds through the foothills of the leeward Koʻolau Range. It starts at Helemano Military Reservation near the Poamoho Ridge hike and finishes by the end of Pūpūkea Rd. near the Kaunala hike.

As of June 1993, the Pa'ala'a Uka Pūpūkea Rd. was in excellent condition. You can drive your car to the start of the trail (map point D), thus eliminating about 2.5 miles of road walking.

29 Kawailoa Ridge

Type:	Graded ridge
Length:	11 mi round trip
Elev. Gain:	1,100 ft
Danger:	Low
Suitable for:	Intermediate, Expert
Location:	Leeward Koʻolau Range above Haleʻiwa
Topo Map:	Hauʻula
Access:	Conditional; open only to outdoor clubs and organizations with permission. Contact Waialua Sugar Co. (phone 637–3521) and the Directorate of Facilities Engineering, U.S. Army Support Command, Fort Shafter, HI 96858.

Trailhead Directions

At Punchbowl St. get on the Lunalilo Fwy (H-1) heading ʻewa (west).

Near Middle St. keep left on Rte 78 west (exit 19B, Moanalua Rd.) to ʻAiea.

By Aloha Stadium bear right to rejoin H-1 to Pearl City.

Take the H-2 freeway (exit 8A) to Wahiawā.

As the freeway ends, continue on Rte 99 north (Wilikina Dr.) bypassing Wahiawā.

Pass Schofield Barracks on the left.

The road narrows to two lanes, dips, and then forks. Take the right fork to Haleʻiwa (Kamananui Rd., but still Rte 99 north).

At the road end turn left on Kamehameha Hwy.

Pass Dole Plantation on the right.

In Weed Circle, bear right into Haleʻiwa town (still Kamehameha Hwy, but now Rte 83).

Cross Anahulu River on a narrow bridge and pass Haleʻiwa Beach Park on the left.

Turn right on Kawailoa Dr. It's the first paved road on the right after the beach park.

Pass Kawailoa Refuse Transfer Station on the left.

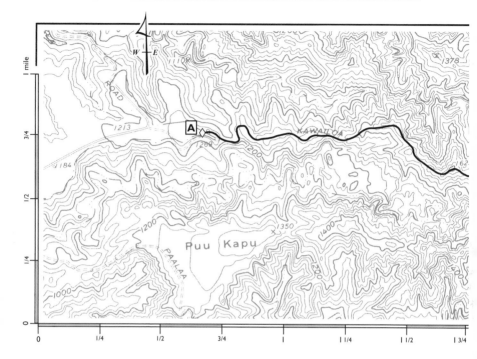

Cross a cane haul road and switchback once to the left.

Just before the second house on the right, turn right on a dirt road. The intersection is marked by a sign "Army Vehicles Detour Here."

Almost immediately reach a locked gate.

Join Kawailoa Rd., a paved cane road.

Ascend gradually through the cane fields. The pavement comes and goes.

By a lone pole reach the junction with Paʻalaʻa Uka Pūpūkea Rd., used by the military. Bear left on it. (To the right the road leads to the trailheads of the Kawainui, Kawai Iki, and ʻŌpaeʻula hikes.)

As the military road turns sharp left (almost back on itself), keep right on a narrower cane road.

The road forks. Keep right again.

Reach the forest reserve boundary. Park there in a small grassy area on the right (map point A).

Route Description

Take the dirt road leading into the forest.

It descends initially and then climbs to gain the ridge line.

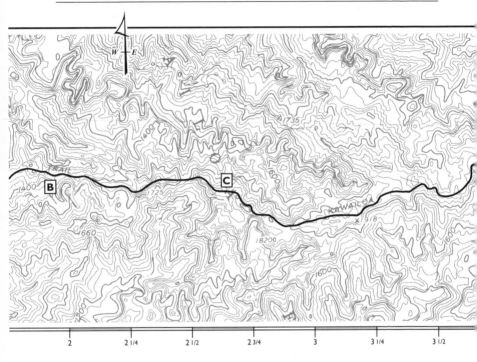

After a long series of ups and downs reach the end of the road at a small grassy turnaround.

Continue straight on a trail that descends steeply and then levels off.

As the trail begins to climb and peter out, reach the junction with the Kawailoa Ridge Trail (map point B). Turn left on it.

Contour on the left side of the ridge below its top.

After a short uluhe fern tunnel, cross over to the right side.

Bear right past a small clearing in the forest.

Switch to the left side of the ridge.

Cross over to the right side for a brief stretch through strawberry guava and koa.

Switch back to the left side (map point C). The trail remains on that side all the way to the summit. Periodically the trail reaches the ridge top at the dips between the hills.

On the right pass a shortcut of a long bend in the trail.

Pass a landslide on the right.

Go through a grove of Australian tea.

In a smaller grove reach an open area with a good view of the summit in the distance.

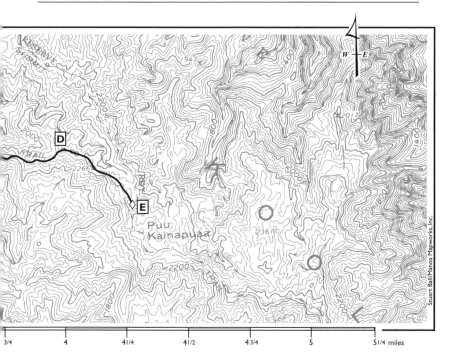

Pass another landslide.

The vegetation thins, and the trail contours close to the ridge top.

Pass three landslides, one above, one below, and one across the trail (map point D).

Go through another grove of Australian tea.

Reach a junction marked by a metal grating. Continue straight, up a flat-topped mound. (To the left the Kawailoa Ridge Trail contours around the mound and ends at the junction with the Ko'olau Summit Trail.)

Reach the Ko'olau summit at the top of the mound, which is occasionally used as a helipad (elev. 2,360 ft) (map point E). On its windward side is a collapsed wooden platform.

Notes

Notice how many times landslides are mentioned in the narrative? Kawailoa is a bear of a hike through extremely wild and rugged terrain. It provides few rewards, but if you like solitude and a challenge, go for it.

The entire trip is for experienced hikers only. Do the hike during the summer when the days are longer, and the weather is drier. Start early because you'll need every hour of daylight. Intermediates can go as far as they like.

From the top you can see Lāʻie and Hauʻula to windward. On the leeward side is the north shore from Kaʻena Point to Haleʻiwa. In the background is the Waiʻanae Range. All around is the jumbled topography of the northern Koʻolau Range.

The Kawailoa Ridge Trail receives little or no maintenance. As a result, it is heavily overgrown with uluhe ferns and *Clidemia* in the lower and middle sections. The upper section near the summit is usually open, as is the road approach.

Although basically graded, the trail has many uneven spots because of erosion and landslides. Watch your footing all the time. Expect to fall down and get muddy and wet.

There is a good variety of native plants on the upper section. You can also see some of the common native birds there.

The strawberry guavas usually ripen in August and September.

The Koʻolau Summit Trail is a graded footpath that winds along the crest of the Koʻolau Range from the end of Pūpūkea Rd to the end of the Kīpapa Ridge Trail. To get to the Lāʻie Trail along the summit, descend the windward side of the mound into a bowl-shaped depression. Go through a grove of Australian tea and cross a marshy area on a metal grating. Climb out of the depression and turn left on the Koʻolau Summit Trail. Up Kawailoa, along the summit, and down Lāʻie makes a superb Koʻolau traverse. Make sure you can recognize the Koʻolau Summit-Lāʻie Trail junction, or you will be spending the night out.

To get to the Poamoho Ridge Trail and points south, walk along the top of the mound to the right. The Koʻolau Summit Trail will be below you on the left. Turn right on it.

The Paʻalaʻa Uka Pūpūkea Rd. is a military thoroughfare that winds through the foothills of the leeward Koʻolau Range. It starts at Helemano Military Reservation near the Poamoho Ridge hike and finishes by the end of Pūpūkea Rd. near the Kaunala hike.

30 Kaunala

Type:	Foothill
Length:	6 mi loop
Elev. Gain:	400 ft
Danger:	Low
Suitable for:	Novice, Intermediate
Location:	Windward Koʻolau Range above Pūpūkea
Topo Map:	Waimea, Kahuku
Access:	Conditional; open on weekends and Federal holidays only.

Trailhead Directions

At Punchbowl St. get on the Lunalilo Fwy (H-1) heading ʻewa (west).

Near Middle St. keep left on Rte 78 west (exit 19B, Moanalua Rd.) to ʻAiea.

By Aloha Stadium bear right to rejoin H-1 to Pearl City.

Take the H-2 freeway (exit 8A) to Wahiawā.

As the freeway ends, continue on Rte 99 north (Wilikina Dr.) bypassing Wahiawā.

Pass Schofield Barracks on the left.

The road narrows to two lanes, dips, and then forks. Take the right fork to Haleʻiwa (Kamananui Rd., but still Rte 99 north).

At the road end turn left on Kamehameha Hwy.

Pass Dole Plantation on the right.

In Weed Circle, bear right into Haleʻiwa town (still Kamehameha Hwy, but now Rte 83).

Cross Anahulu River on a narrow bridge and proceed up the north shore.

Go around Waimea Bay, passing Waimea Falls Park on the right.

By Foodland Supermarket turn right on Pūpūkea Rd. That's the first major intersection after the bay.

Switchback once up a small pali.

Drive to the end of the paved road at Camp Pūpūkea, a Boy Scout camp (map point A).

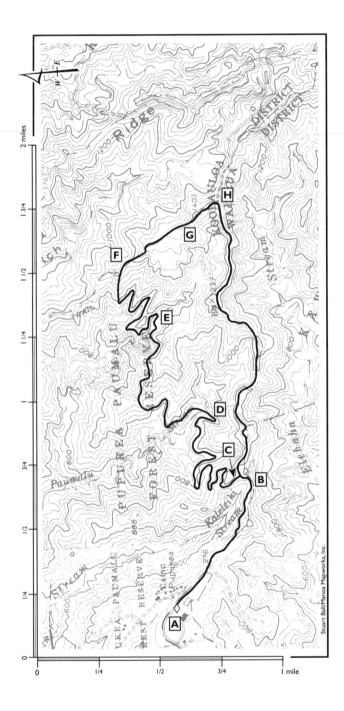

Park off the road. Leave plenty of room for vehicles exiting the camp and the farm across the street.

Route Description

Proceed along the dirt road past the Boy Scout camp.

Climb over a locked gate and enter the Kahuku Range, an Army training area.

Pass an abandoned cattle loading ramp on the right in a grove of ironwoods.

Reach a junction (map point B). Keep left on the main road. (The dirt road to the right through a locked gate is the Pa'ala'a Uka Pūpūkea Rd.)

Shortly afterward pass a small concrete culvert on the right.

Approach a large grove of paperbark trees.

At its edge turn left on a wide path, which is the Kaunala Trail (map point C).

The path splits almost immediately. Take the left fork. (The right fork goes up a hill.)

Contour around the hill covered with paperbark trees.

Descend gradually on four switchbacks. Ignore trails going straight down the side ridges.

Contour in and out of several gulches.

The first one is long and narrow.

Descend on two short switchbacks to the second one, which has a tiny stream (map point D).

The fifth gulch is larger and has a good-sized stream (map point E).

After crossing a small stream in the next gulch, reach a sunny open area covered with uluhe ferns.

Climb a side ridge on its right side.

Switchback once and reach a junction with a dirt road in a grove of paperbark trees (map point F). Turn right on the road. (To the left it leads down to Camp Paumalū, a Girl Scout camp. Across the road Kaunala Trail extended continues.)

Climb steadily along a ridge. Keep to the main road.

Reach a flat cleared area (elev. 1,403 ft) (map point G). From it is a good view of the Wai'anae Range and the north shore.

Descend steeply, but briefly.

Reach a junction with a wider dirt road near a stand of Norfolk Island pines (map point H). Turn right on it. (To the left the road heads mauka to the start [end] of the Ko'olau Summit Trail.)

In the grove of paperbark trees reach the junction with the Kaunala Trail (map point C).

Retrace your steps to the Boy Scout camp (map point A).

Notes

This hike is an easy valley-ridge combination. The Kaunala Trail winds through the lush gulches of the Pūpūkea Paumalū Forest Reserve. The return route follows a ridge top through the Army's Kahuku training area.

The Kaunala Trail receives regular maintenance and is thus usually clear.

The gulches can be muddy and mosquitoey.

Kaunala extended is a rough, unimproved trail that starts across the road from the end of the official Kaunala Trail. After about 1.5 miles the extension emerges onto the main dirt road. Turn right on the road to return to Camp Pūpūkea. The first left on the way back is the start (end) of the Koʻolau Summit Trail.

The Summit Trail is a graded footpath that winds along the crest of the Koʻolau Range from the end of Pūpūkea Rd. to the end of the Kīpapa Ridge Trail. The trail is for experienced hikers only because it is overgrown, muddy, and sometimes narrow and obscure.

Access to Kaunala extended or the Koʻolau Summit Trail requires written permission from the Directorate of Facilities Engineering, U.S. Army Support Command, Fort Shafter, HI 96858.

The Paʻalaʻa Uka Pūpūkea Rd. is a military thoroughfare that winds through the foothills of the leeward Koʻolau Range. It starts at Helemano Military Reservation near the Poamoho Ridge hike and finishes near the end of Pūpūkea Rd. on this hike.

WAIMĀNALO TO KAʻAʻAWA

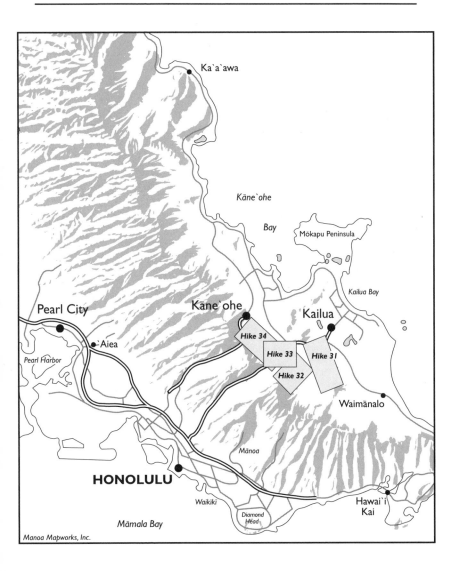

Manoa Mapworks, Inc.

31 Olomana

Type:	Ungraded ridge
Length:	5 mi round trip
Elev. Gain:	1,600 ft
Danger:	High
Suitable for:	Intermediate, Expert
Location:	Windward Koʻolau Range above Maunawili
Topo Map:	Mōkapu, Koko Head
Access:	Conditional; open to individuals and organized groups with verbal permission. Call the Y. Y. Valley Corp. (phone 261–1437) or the Royal Hawaiian Country Club (phone 532–1440).

Trailhead Directions

At Punchbowl St. get on the Pali Hwy (Rte 61 north) heading up Nuʻuanu Valley.

Go under the Pali through the twin tunnels.

The Pali Hwy becomes Kalanianaʻole Hwy at the first traffic light.

At the third traffic light turn right on Aʻuloa Rd.

Almost immediately turn left on an unnamed road that parallels the highway.

Park on the side of the road just before it crosses a bridge over Maunawili Stream (map point A).

Route Description

Continue along the unnamed road on foot.

Just after crossing the bridge, turn right on a paved road marked by two wooden posts.

Almost immediately the road forks. Keep right on the paved road paralleling the stream.

At a second fork, bear right through a gate (map point B).

Cross a bridge and begin climbing.

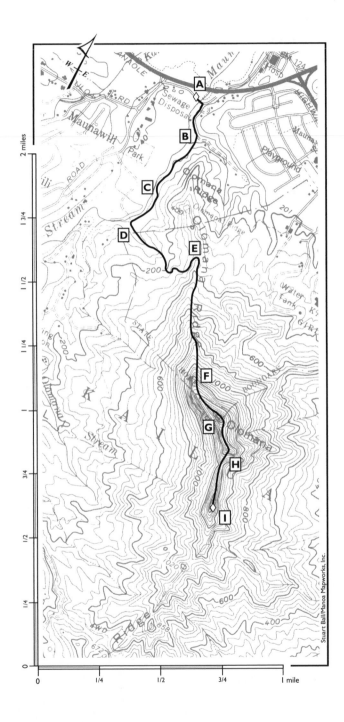

After the road levels off, pass two small drainage shafts with grates on top.

After the road bears left, pass a concrete and rock culvert on the left.

Twenty yards beyond the culvert turn left on a trail by a large boulder (map point C).

Climb briefly, first on two switchbacks and then straight up.

Bear right and begin contouring along the side of the ridge.-

Go through a bamboo grove.

Break out into the open briefly and then enter a grove of strawberry guava and Christmas berry.

After a short rise reach a dirt road (map point D). That junction is marked by a metal gate post. Turn left on the road heading uphill.

Ascend gradually alongside a small gully.

Cross the gully by an abandoned pumping shack.

Work left, climbing steadily up the side of the ridge.

Gain the ridge line at a small dip marked by a metal gate and a utility pole (map point E).

Turn right, up the ridge, on a trail.

Cross two eroded sections and enter an ironwood grove.

Gradually ascend the flank of the mountain through a corridor of Christmas berry.

Begin climbing more steeply (map point F).

Go to the right up a long rock face partially covered by vegetation. A cable there provides some assistance.

The angle of ascent decreases markedly for a short stretch below the summit.

Climb a small, but nearly vertical rock face with the aid of a cable.

The ridge narrows considerably.

Bear right off the ridge line to avoid an especially narrow section.

Reach the summit of the first peak (elev. 1,643 ft) (map point G) at a rocky outcrop.

Descend steeply through grass to a saddle and climb briefly to the second peak (map point H).

Just past its summit turn sharp right down off the ridge.

Descend precipitously to the saddle between the second and third peaks. A very long cable provides assistance there.

Begin climbing the very thin ridge of the third peak.

Inch left around a large boulder with a hole in it. A cable provides some security.

Scramble up a long rock face with the aid of another cable.

Keep left around a large free-standing boulder.

Bear right off the ridge line and climb the final rock face with the help of still another cable.

Reach the flat summit of the third peak (map point I).

Notes

Olomana is an awe-inspiring, alluring mountain. From a distance it looks unclimbable. Olomana is Oʻahu's version of the Matterhorn.

At the top of the first peak is a 360-degree panorama. Makai is the windward coast from Makapuʻu to Kualoa points. Mauka is Maunawili Valley and the Koʻolau Range. The massive peak to the left of the Pali is Kōnā-huanui, the highest point in the Koʻolau Range. Try picking out the other major peaks on the summit ridge. They are, from left to right, Puʻu o Kona, Lanipō, and Mt. Olympus.

The climb to the first and second peaks is an intermediate hike with medium danger. A short section just below the first peak is narrow, and there is a rock face that must be negotiated. The descent from the second peak and the ascent to the third peak are for experienced hikers only. The rock is loose, and the ridge plunges straight down on both sides. Take your time and be extraordinarily careful. Test all cables before using them.

The trail receives periodic maintenance. It overgrows slowly between clearings and is thus usually open.

32 Koʻolaupoko

Type:	Foothill
Length:	5 mi round trip
Elev. Gain:	600 ft
Danger:	Low
Suitable for:	Novice, Intermediate
Location:	Windward Koʻolau Range above Maunawili
Topo Map:	Koko Head, Honolulu
Access:	Open

Trailhead Directions

At Punchbowl St. get on the Pali Hwy (Rte 61 north) heading up Nuʻuanu Valley.

Go under the Pali through the twin tunnels.

The Pali Hwy becomes Kalanianaʻole Hwy at the first traffic light.

At the third traffic light turn right on Aʻuloa Rd.

Almost immediately the road forks. Keep left on Maunawili Rd. It passes through Maunawili subdivision and then narrows through a forested area.

As the subdivision reappears, turn right on Aloha ʻOe Dr.

Take the third right on Lopaka Pl.

At the top of the hill reach the intersection with Lopaka Way.

Park on the street near that intersection (map point A).

Route Description

Proceed up Lopaka Way on foot.

Go through a locked gate.

The road switchbacks four times and then ends at a Board of Water Supply tank (map point B).

Bear left along the perimeter fence of the tank.

At the far corner turn right and continue to hug the fence.

As the path (and fence) begin to descend, turn left on a trail heading upslope.

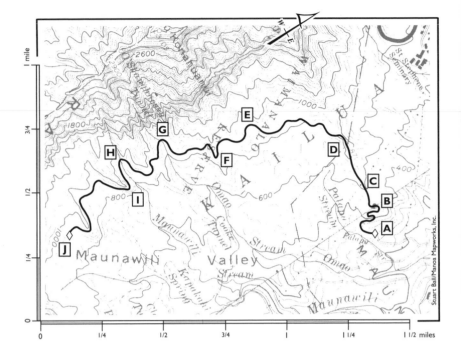

Shortly afterward reach the top of the ridge and a junction. Turn right on the Piliwale Ridge Trail.

Climb gradually along the ridge.

In an open area a dirt road comes in on the right (map point C). Continue straight up to some power-line poles.

Pass a second set of poles.

Climb steadily through guava and uluhe ferns.

The ridge levels off momentarily.

Resume the ascent.

Descend gradually and then more steeply.

Reach the junction with the wide Maunawili Trail (map point D). Turn left on it. (Straight ahead the ridge trail leads to the base of the Ko'olau cliffs. To the right, the Maunawili Trail and a short connector trail lead down to the hairpin turn on Pali Hwy.

Begin contouring across the slopes of the Ko'olau foothills.

Break out into the open through uluhe ferns. Mauka are spectacular views of the Ko'olau cliffs.

Enter another gulch and then emerge into the open again.

Work into and out of a series of shallow gulches.

Cross a wide rocky stream bed (map point E).

Cross another stream bed.

Cross over a broad side ridge with a stand of ironwood trees above and on the right.

Work into and out of another gulch and then cross over a narrow, open side ridge (map point F). From it are views of the Ko'olau Range from Makapu'u Point to Kōnāhuanui.

Descend into a deep gulch on two switchbacks.

Contour through a series of shallow gulches.

Cross three rocky stream beds right in a row. At the second one a side trail to the right leads to the base of a waterfall chute and the O'Shaughnessy Tunnel.

Descend into a deep, narrow gulch.

Cross intermittent 'Ōma'o Stream by a stand of bamboo (map point G). A faint side trail leads upstream to Smiling Falls. It is named for the shape of the rock dike at its base.

Contour through another small gulch and then cross over an open side ridge with two ironwoods on the right.

Descend into a large gulch on two switchbacks.

Cross Maunawili Stream (map point H).

Climb to the next side ridge (map point I). It has a dirt bench on the right and great views.

Work in and out of two more gulches.

Pass a lone palm tree on the right.

An old koa tree arches gracefully above the trail.

In the next gulch, the improved trail ended (map point J) until construction in 1992 carried the trail 2.25 miles farther toward Waimānalo.

Notes

Maunawili is O'ahu's newest trail. Richard H. (Dick) Davis of the Hawaiian Trail and Mountain Club scouted the route. Construction started in the summer of 1991 and will continue through 1995. Volunteer crews under the sponsorship of the Hawai'i Service Trip Program of the Sierra Club completed 3 miles in 1991 and 2.25 miles in 1992. As of October 1992, the improved trail ran from above the hairpin turn on the Pali Hwy for 5.25 miles toward Waimānalo. The sections remaining to be constructed are from the Pali lookout to above the hairpin turn and from the current end to Anianinui Ridge near Waimānalo.

The route described uses the Piliwale Ridge Trail as access and then follows the Maunawili Trail. The ridge trail is brushy and occasionally steep. Don't be discouraged, however, because Maunawili is wide, open, and well graded.

Easier access is available from the hairpin turn on the Pali Hwy. Park in the small lot on the right just past the turn. A short connector trail leaves from the parking lot and climbs to the Maunawili Trail. Turn left on it and pick up the description at the intersection with the Piliwale Ridge Trail.

The views from the open sections of the Maunawili Trail are breathtaking. Makai is Olomana with its three peaks. Beyond are Kailua and Waimānalo bays. Mauka loom the fluted cliffs of the Ko'olau summit range. Along it you can see the peaks of Pu'u o Kona, Lanipō, Mt. Olympus, and Kōnāhuanui.

If you are caught out in a heavy rain storm, look up. Every notch in the Ko'olau cliffs will have a waterfall. Be careful on the stream crossings.

Memorize the junction of the Maunawili and Piliwale Ridge Trails for the return trip. Also note the junction in back of the water tank.

Access to Piliwale Ridge will be rerouted some time in the future. The new trail will leave from the far right corner of the water tank and contour along the side of the ridge to the dirt road. You will then turn left on the road to reach the power-line poles and the ridge trail.

A short section of the Maunawili Trail on the Waimānalo side is somewhat improved and makes a great novice hike. To get to it, enter Waimānalo from the Pali side and turn right on Kumuhau St. At the stop sign turn right on Waikupanaha St. and cross a bridge. Look for a house on the left with a blue metal roof (no. 41-1020). Park on the street near it.

Proceed up the Old Government Rd., which is the dirt road across from the house. Bear left and up at the first fork. The road narrows to a trail as it ascends gradually toward Anianinui Ridge. By a large mango tree, reach the junction with the Maunawili Trail. Turn left on it and go as far as you like. The Old Government Rd. continues straight past some boulders blocking vehicle access.

The Maunawili Trail used to be named the Ko'olaupoko Trail.

Hanauma Bay and Koko Crater. (Photo by Jason Sunada.)

Mānoa Falls and pool. ʻAihualama-ʻŌhiʻa hike. (Photo by John Hoover.)

Second and third peaks.
Olomana hike. (Photo by
John Hoover.)

On the trail. Pu'u Kalena
hike. (Photo by John
Hoover.)

'Ōhi'a tree. Kānehoa-
Hāpapa hike. (Photo by
John Hoover.)

In the gulch. Ma'akua Gulch
hike. (Photo by Albert
Miller.)

Climbing the narrow dike. Pu'u Kalena hike. (Photo by John Hoover.)

Hiker in the mist. Pu'u Manamana hike. (Photo by John Hoover.)

Sheer ridge. Pu'u Manamana hike. (Photo by Jason Sunada.)

Up the waterfall. Ka'au Crater hike. (Photo by John Hoover.)

Rainbow in Koʻiahi Gulch. ʻŌhikilolo hike. (Photo by Jason Sunada.)

Kolekole Pass: peaks of Puʻu Hāpapa, Puʻu Kānehoa, Puʻu Kaua, and Palikea. Puʻu Kalena hike. (Photo by John Hoover.)

Ridge route, Mākua Valley. ʻŌhikilolo hike. (Photo by John Hoover.)

Koʻolau cliffs, Kōnāhuanui in back. Kuliʻouʻou Ridge hike. (Photo by John Hoover.)

Kahana Valley. Kahana Valley hike. (Photo by John Hoover.)

Pu'u 'Ōhulehule. Schofield-Waikāne hike. (Photo by Albert Miller.)

33 Old Pali Road

Type: Foothill

Length: 3 mi round trip

Elev. Gain: 500 ft

Danger: Low

Suitable for: Novice

Location: Windward Ko'olau Range below Nu'uanu Pali

Topo Map: Honolulu, Kāne'ohe

Access: Open

Trailhead Directions

At Punchbowl St. get on the Pali Hwy (Rte 61 north) heading up Nu'uanu Valley.

Just before the tunnels, turn right to the Pali lookout.

Enter Nu'uanu Pali State Park.

Park in the lot (map point A).

Route Description

Walk to the Pali lookout (elev. 1,200 ft).

Turn right down the ramp to the Old Pali Rd.

Climb around to the left of a black gate.

Descend gradually along the paved road, which narrows to one lane several times.

Just before the road switchbacks left, reach the junction with the unimproved section of the Maunawili Trail (map point B). Continue briefly along the road until it is blocked by the Pali Hwy.

Go around the end of the fence on the right and drop down below the main highway.

Squeeze through a narrow passageway underneath the Kailua-bound lanes.

Go under the Honolulu-bound lanes on a much wider walkway.

Pick up the Old Pali Rd. again, now much overgrown with grass.

Descend gradually, working back toward the Nu'uanu Pali.

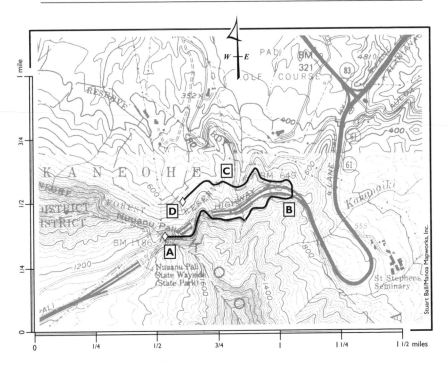

Walk under three supports for the Honolulu-bound lanes of the highway.

The grass ends, and the pavement of the old road reappears.

Reach the junction with Aʻuloa Rd. Bear left on it.

Look for a short concrete wall on the left before the road curves right.

Just past the wall and by a metal post, turn left up some stone steps, partially hidden by vegetation (map point C).

The steps become a trail leading up the right side of a small gulch.

Climb the right side of the gulch on several short switchbacks.

Reach the top of a side ridge.

Cross over it and bear left down the other side.

Contour along the side of the ridge on a sometimes narrow trail.

It eventually widens and descends through a grove of white-barked albizia trees.

Just after the grove and before the trail begins to climb through heavy forest, turn right and down on a wide, but grassy trail.

Pass several large mango trees.

Descend gradually through a series of hau groves.

Climb briefly along the edge of a hau grove.

Cross a small stream and turn left upstream. Almost immediately reach a waterfall with a tiny pool at its base (map point D). The path heading down through the hau is the Likeke Trail.

Notes

This hike is a pleasant half-day walk to a small waterfall below the Pali lookout. The hike follows the old road down from the Nu'uanu Pali. Imagine what an adventure it was to drive a small car on this narrow, tortuous, windy road!

Views along the Old Pali Rd. are excellent. You can see Kāne'ohe and Kailua bays. Olomana is the triple-peaked mountain standing by itself. Looking back toward the lookout, you can see the peak of Lanihuli on the right. Towering above you is Kōnāhuanui (elev. 3,150), the highest peak in the Ko'olau Range.

The trail receives periodic maintenance. It overgrows between clearings.

You can combine the Old Pali Rd. and Likeke hikes, if you have two cars. Park one on Likelike Hwy and the other at the Pali lookout. The combined hike is about 4 mi long one way. Do it in either direction.

34 Likeke

Type:	Foothill
Length:	5 mi round trip
Elev. Gain:	100 ft
Danger:	Low
Suitable for:	Intermediate
Location:	Windward Koʻolau Range above Kāneʻohe
Topo Map:	Honolulu, Kāneʻohe
Access:	Open

Trailhead Directions

At Punchbowl St. get on the Lunalilo Fwy (H-1) heading ʻewa (west).

Take Likelike Hwy (exit 20A, Rte 63 north) up Kalihi Valley through the Wilson Tunnel.

After exiting the tunnel, pass a closed-off parking lot on the right.

Continue down Likelike Hwy for about 0.3 mi. Park off the highway on the grass near an emergency call box (map point A).

Route Description

Walk back up Likelike Hwy to the closed-off parking lot.

At its far end turn left on to the Likeke Trail (map point B).

Descend gradually through the forest.

Reach an overgrown junction (map point C). Turn right and begin contouring along the slope.

Descend into the first gulch. Cross the stream bed, walk up the gulch briefly, and then climb out.

Contour through a long stretch of hala trees and then uluhe ferns.

Work down a deep gulch, first on one side of the stream bed and then on the other. Climb steeply out of the gulch.

Descend a side ridge past a spreading mango tree.

Turn right in a hala grove overlooking a golf course.

Cross a small stream bed near a stand of bamboo.

Cross a wide, rocky stream bed.

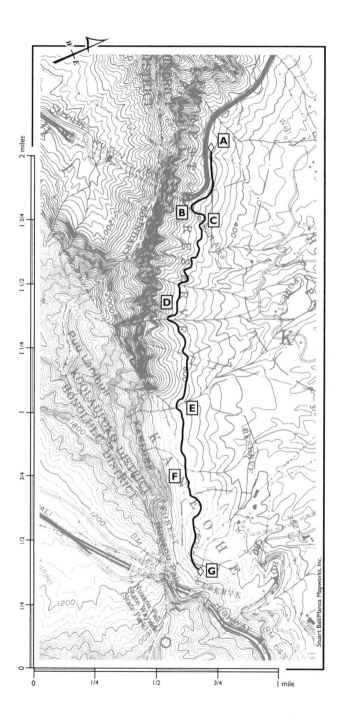

Work into and out of a large gulch.

Contour through an open mixed forest.

Cross a small gulch with hau tangles.

Pass a mango tree on the left.

Enter a hala grove and then traverse an open area with uluhe ferns.

Descend into a large gulch between two mango trees (map point D). Walk up the gulch briefly and then cross the stream below a small waterfall. Ascend out of the gulch through a grove of kukui trees.

Work into and out of another gulch with a tiny pool and hala trees.

Descend into a narrow gulch through uluhe. Walk up the gulch briefly and cross the stream bed. Pass a mango tree on the climb out of the gulch.

Descend into a deep gulch on two short switchbacks (map point E). Work down the gulch briefly and then climb out of it.

Pass a mango tree on the right.

Cross a large gulch, dark with guava trees (map point F).

Cross a smaller, steeper gulch.

Skirt to the right of a series of large mango trees.

Cross a broken rock wall and pass a large mango tree on the right.

Contour across a gentle hillside through mixed forest.

Work along the edge of a hau grove.

Cross a small gulch and then enter a hau grove.

Keep to the right across two partially open areas.

Climb a small gully filled with hau.

Reach a small waterfall (map point G). There the Likeke Trail ends. The trail to the left across a small stream leads to the Old Pali Rd. and is part of that hike.

Notes

The Likeke hike contours below the windward Ko'olau cliffs between the Wilson and Pali Tunnels. The trail works in and out of numerous deep, dark, lush gulches. The path, however, is rough and mostly unimproved. Try the Old Pali Rd. hike first. It goes through similar country but is much easier.

There are some views from the open sections of the trail. You can see Kailua and Kāne'ohe bays. Olomana is the triple-peaked mountain on the right. Ho'omaluhia Park lies makai of the H-3 freeway. Mauka are the near-vertical cliffs of the Ko'olau Range.

Parts of the trail are hard to follow. Remember that it cuts across the topography while maintaining about the same elevation. The trail sometimes goes up or down a gulch or ridge but only for a short period of time. Do not be diverted by the numerous side trails heading straight up or down.

There are lots of mosquitoes on this hike.

The trail receives sporadic maintenance. The sections through hau and uluhe overgrow between clearings.

You can combine the Likeke and Old Pali Rd. hikes if you have two cars. Park one on Likelike Hwy and the other at the Pali lookout. The combined hike is about 4 mi long one way. Do it in either direction.

Windward Ko'olau Range

KAHANA TO LĀ'IE

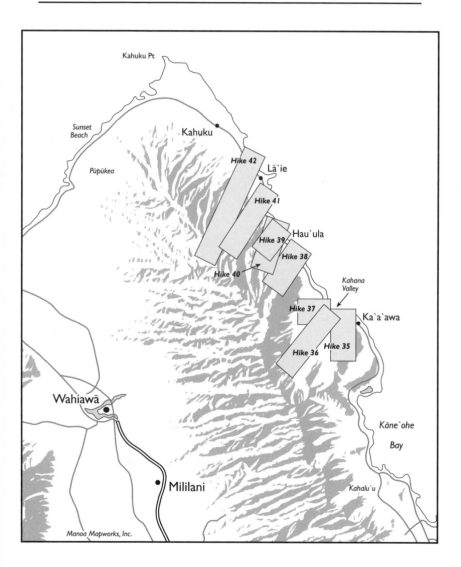

Kahuku Pt

Sunset
Beach

Kahuku

Pūpūkea

Hike 42

Lā`ie

Hike 41

Hau`ula

Hike 39

Hike 38

Hike 40

Kahana
Valley

Hike 37

Ka`a`awa

Hike 35

Hike 36

Wahiawā

Kāne`ohe

Bay

Mililani

Kahalu`u

Manoa Mapworks, Inc.

35 Pu'u Manamana

Type:	Ungraded ridge
Length:	4 mi loop
Elev. Gain:	2,100 ft
Danger:	High
Suitable for:	Expert
Location:	Windward Ko'olau Range above Kahana Bay
Topo Map:	Kahana
Access:	Open

Trailhead Directions

At Punchbowl St. get on the Lunalilo Fwy (H-1) heading 'ewa (west).

Take Likelike Hwy (exit 20A, Rte 63 north) up Kalihi Valley through the Wilson Tunnel.

Turn left on Kahekili Hwy (Rte 83 west). That junction is the first major one after the tunnel and is marked Kahalu'u—Lā'ie.

Kahekili Hwy becomes Kamehameha Hwy (still Rte 83), which continues up the windward coast.

Drive through the villages of Kahalu'u and Waiāhole to Ka'a'awa.

Pass Swanzy Beach Park on the right and the Crouching Lion Inn on the left.

The road curves left to skirt Kahana Bay.

Park on the right shoulder just before the road turns right and crosses Kahana Stream (map point A). The spot is near a bus stop and a plaque set in a rock.

Route Description

Walk back along Kamehameha Hwy toward Crouching Lion Inn.

Pass a house on the right.

Look for a short guard rail on the right with a Rte 83 sign near it.

At the first utility pole past the guard rail, turn right into the forest (map point B). Across the road from the turn is a line of ironwood trees.

Climb straight up the hillside on an indistinct trail through ti plants.

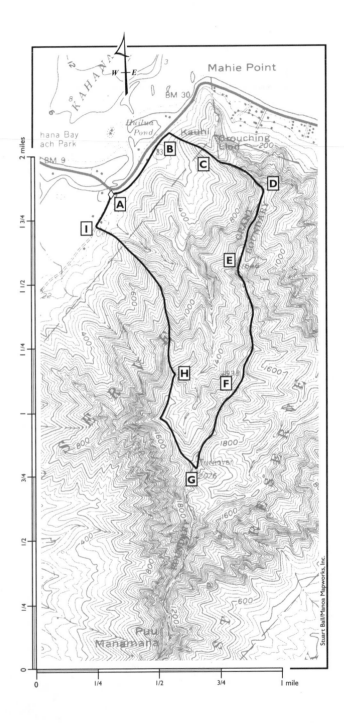

As the hill levels off, bear left through tangled Christmas berry.

Ascend gradually through scattered ti plants.

Bear right through another Christmas berry tangle.

Work left, climbing steadily on the trail, now well defined.

Switchback to the right and then to the left across a rocky outcrop.

Turn right and begin climbing straight up the ridge.

Break out into the open in a grassy area.

The ridge levels off briefly (map point C). Look to the left for a view of the Crouching Lion rock formation.

Resume serious climbing.

Cross a narrow rocky neck.

Ascend very steeply past several rock faces. There are two cables for assistance.

Reach the main ridge line with its views toward Kāne'ohe (map point D).

Bear right along the main ridge heading mauka.

Enter a small Christmas berry grove and then cross two eroded spots.

Climb steadily, mostly over rock, to a pointed peak. There is one cable for assistance.

After a level section go right, around a rock face, with the aid of a cable.

Descend a steep rock face with the help of a cable.

Climb steadily, first over rock, and then through mixed forest.

Pass a small overlook on the right with views of Kahana Valley (map point E).

Descend steeply and then negotiate another rock face with the aid of two cables.

Climb steeply on the narrow ridge. Be careful in this section. The vegetation provides some security, but the ridge is still very narrow.

As the ridge widens, enter native forest with 'ōhi'a, 'ie'ie, and uluhe ferns.

Climb briefly to a knob on the ridge.

Descend and then climb steeply to a second knob.

Ascend gradually to a third knob (map point F).

Descend briefly and then climb moderately to a broad knob.

Descend and then climb to a smaller knob.

Traverse a wet level section. The ridge is quite broad here, and the trail works from side to side following the easiest route.

Pass a small open space with a nice updraft from the back of Hidden Valley.

Climb moderately to a broad knob called Turnover (elev. 2,027 ft).

Along its top reach a junction (map point G). Continue straight to a clearing with a benchmark. (The trail to the right and down is the return portion of the loop.)

From the clearing backtrack to the junction and turn left down the side ridge.

Descend, steeply at first, and then more gradually along the ridge. Keep to its left side.

Cross a level wet section interspersed with several muddy dips.

Climb briefly to a small knob (map point H).

Resume the descent as the ridge begins to narrow.

Cross a short level section.

Descend very steeply on the ever-narrowing ridge.

The ridge becomes razor thin. Short stretches are carpeted with moss.

Finally, the ridge widens, but the descent remains steep.

Descend a narrow rocky section.

Go left around a rock outcropping with the help of a cable.

Descend steeply through a hala grove.

Reach a small cemetery in the forest.

Take the main path down through the graveyard.

Emerge on to a lawn by an old Mormon chapel.

Reach dirt Trout Farm Rd. and turn right on it (map point I).

Cross a small bridge.

Reach Kamehameha Hwy directly across from the bus stop and plaque (map point A).

Notes

Pu'u Manamana is one of the most dangerous hikes on the island. This loop is for expert hikers only. It becomes difficult right at the start and then gets worse.

The narrow sections along the main ridge are legendary. The rock is loose and crumbly. Be very careful. Test all cables before using them. There is no shame in turning back if you don't like what you see.

The return portion of the loop is also very narrow and steep. You drop over 2,000 ft in a little over a mile. The ridge is forested, so you can use the trees for support. Again, be careful.

The views are well worth the climb. Makai is the windward coast from Lā'ie Point to Makapu'u Point. From the main ridge you can see Kahana Bay and Valley. The massive peak across the valley is Pu'u Piei.

At the Turnover clearing, Punalu'u Valley is on the right beyond Kahana. Ka'a'awa Valley is on the left. Pu'u Manamana and Pu'u 'Ōhulehule are straight ahead. In the distance is the long Ko'olau summit ridge. Look for the 'ōhi'a with the yellow blossoms at the edge of the clearing.

The Pu'u Manamana loop receives sporadic maintenance. The middle section before and after Turnover overgrows rapidly between clearings. The front section going up and the lower section going down are usually open.

The Pu'u Manamana hike is also known as Crouching Lion or Turnover.

36 Kahana Valley

Type:	Valley
Length:	8 mi double loop
Elev. Gain:	400 ft
Danger:	Low
Suitable for:	Novice, Intermediate
Location:	Windward Koʻolau Range in back of Kahana Bay
Topo Map:	Kahana, Hauʻula
Access:	Open

Trailhead Directions

At Punchbowl St. get on the Lunalilo Fwy (H-1) heading ʻewa (west).

Take Likelike Hwy (exit 20A, Rte 63 north) up Kalihi Valley through the Wilson Tunnel.

Turn left on Kahekili Hwy (Rte 83 west). That junction is the first major one after the tunnel and is marked Kahaluʻu—Lāʻie.

Kahekili Hwy becomes Kamehameha Hwy (still Rte 83), which continues up the windward coast.

Drive through the villages of Kahaluʻu and Waiāhole to Kaʻaʻawa.

Pass the Crouching Lion Inn on the left.

The road curves left to go around Kahana Bay.

Cross Kahana Stream on a bridge.

Cross another bridge.

By a large palm grove turn left into Kahana Valley State Park.

Look for the visitor center (marked Orientation) on the right. Park there (map point A).

Route Description

Continue along the main park road on foot.

Go around a locked metal gate.

Reach a junction with another dirt road by Kahana Wells I. Continue straight on the main road.

As the road curves right and up, bear left on a narrow dirt road (map point B). That junction is marked by a metal gate across the paved road and a faded forest reserve sign for hunters. (The paved road is the return leg of the first loop.)

Descend gradually on the eroded road.

Reach Kahana Stream (map point C) and cross it on a small dam by a gauging station. Watch your footing because the top of the dam is very slippery. Nearby is a large swimming hole popular with valley residents.

On the far side turn left on a trail heading downstream.

Turn right, away from the stream and toward the back of the valley.

Climb gradually on a terrace on the side of a ridge.

Gain the ridge line, where the vegetation opens up and the terrain is more level.

Reach a junction in a flat clearing (map point D). Turn right and down off the ridge.

Descend along another terrace through hala and hau.

By a large mango tree reach Kahana Stream again and, shortly afterward, cross it.

Go through another hau grove and then begin climbing along a terrace.

Reach a four-way junction in a clearing surrounded by hala trees (map point E). Turn left and descend along a terrace. (Straight ahead is the return portion of the first loop. To the right is a trail leading back to the main road at the junction marked by the metal gate.)

Shortly afterward, reach a fork (map point F). Take the right fork, which contours above Kahana Stream. (The left fork leads down to Kahana Stream and is the return portion of the second loop.)

Cross a side stream on a slippery rock surface. Just before the crossing is a grove of mountain apples.

Pass a spreading mango tree on the left.

Cross a second side stream by two mango trees.

Reach a junction (map point G). Keep right on the main trail. (The obscure trail on the left leads down to Kahana Stream.)

Cross two more side streams.

Reach a large side stream and another obscure junction (map point H). Continue straight along the side stream. (To the right is the upper trail, which crosses the side stream and continues to the back of the valley. The trail ends at the intake of the Waiāhole ditch.)

Cross the side stream and leave it behind.

Reach Kahana Stream and turn left downstream.

Cross the main stream where it turns sharp left and forms a lovely pool

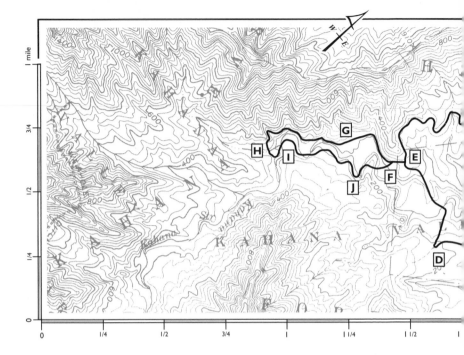

(map point I). The previously mentioned side stream comes in on the left at this point.

Continue downstream on the right bank.

Cross Kahana Stream again.

Cross a side stream coming in on the left.

Cross the main stream by two large albizia trees with white-flecked trunks.

Pass a large mango tree with exposed roots on the opposite side of the stream.

Cross the stream again just before it turns sharp left (map point J). There is a large mango tree and another deep pool nearby.

Continue downstream briefly and reach a junction. Turn right and cross Kahana Stream, which is quite wide at this point. (To the left a short trail leads back to the outgoing portion of the second loop.)

The stream splits briefly. Cross the island in between and then return to the right side.

Cross a small side stream.

Reach a large mango tree and a nice pool.

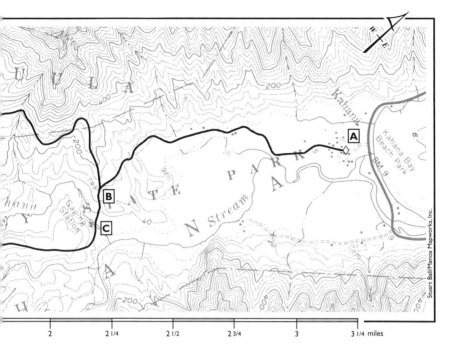

Cross the stream there and enter a bamboo grove on the far side.

Ascend through the grove, leaving the stream for good.

Work left and then straight up the slope on a narrow rutted trail.

Reach the junction with the contour trail (map point F). Keep right.

Reach the four-way junction again (map point E). This time turn left uphill. (If you want to bypass the water tank and more road walking, continue straight across the intersection on the contour trail.)

Climb to a terrace along the side of the valley and contour along it.

Jump across a narrow, but deep, cut.

Reach a huge water tank and turn right along the perimeter fence.

Walk around to the front of the tank and take the paved road.

Reach the original road junction marked by the metal gate (map point B).

Retrace your steps along the main road to the visitor center (map point A).

Notes

This hike is an intriguing double loop in a large, mostly undeveloped valley on the windward side. The long approach leaves something to be desired, but the return portion along the stream is perhaps the most beautiful valley walk on the island. It is not as spectacular as some of the gulch hikes, but the water rushing by is cool and clear, and the pools are deep and inviting. There is really nothing better in life than spending a sunny afternoon by Kahana Stream.

Check in at the visitor center (phone 237–8858 or 237–8266) to get a trail map. You may also be able to get a vehicle permit and the combination to the lock on the first gate. If so, you can drive to the second gate (map point B) and park there. That eliminates about 2.5 miles of road walking.

The variations on this hike are too numerous to mention. For a shorter outing, walk the first loop only. Do, however, take a side trip down to the pools (map points E to F toward J).

Watch your footing while crossing the stream. The rocks can be slippery. Be prepared to get your boots wet and muddy or else wear tabis (Japanese reef walkers). As always, do not attempt the stream crossings if the water is above your knees.

The trail coming back along the stream is not well defined in spots. Remember to keep heading downstream. Look for the bamboo grove on the left because that's where the trail leaves the stream for good.

The trails making up this hike receive periodic maintenance. The contour trail overgrows quickly between clearings. The road approach and the trail along the stream are usually open.

There are some mosquitoes along the stream. Pick a pool with some sun, and you'll avoid most of them.

The mountain apples usually ripen in late July and early August.

The upper trail to the ditch intake at the back of the valley is rough and overgrown. Across the intake is the start (end) of the Waiāhole Ditch Trail, which contours around the back of Kahana, Waikāne, and Waiāhole valleys. Don't venture on it, however, because it is closed to the public.

37 Pu'u Piei

Type:	Ungraded ridge
Length:	2 mi round trip
Elev. Gain:	1,700 ft
Danger:	Medium
Suitable for:	Intermediate
Location:	Windward Ko'olau Range above Kahana Bay
Topo Map:	Kahana
Access:	Open

Trailhead Directions

At Punchbowl St. get on the Lunalilo Fwy (H-1) heading 'ewa (west).

Take Likelike Hwy (exit 20A, Rte 63 north) up Kalihi Valley through the Wilson Tunnel.

Turn left on Kahekili Hwy (Rte 83 west). That junction is the first major one after the tunnel and is marked Kahalu'u-Lā'ie.

Kahekili Hwy becomes Kamehameha Hwy (still Rte 83), which continues up the windward coast.

Drive through the villages of Kahalu'u and Waiāhole to Ka'a'awa.

Pass the Crouching Lion Inn on the left.

The road curves left to go around Kahana Bay.

Cross Kahana Stream on a bridge.

Cross another bridge.

By a large palm grove turn left into Kahana Valley State Park.

Take the first right into a lot and park there (map point A).

Route Description

Walk back to Kamehameha Hwy and turn left toward Punalu'u.

The road curves to the right.

Pass rest rooms on the right.

Pass a boat-launching ramp on the right and a rocky gully on the left.

At the first utility pole (no. 313) past the gully, turn left into the woods on a trail (map point B).

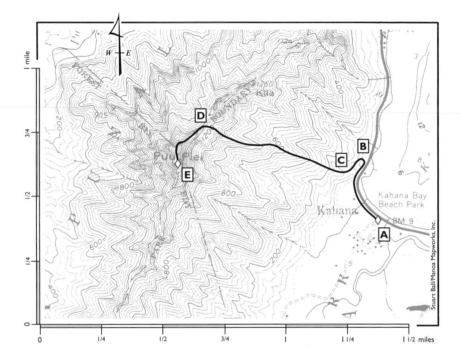

The trail bears right and parallels the road briefly.

Work left up the side of a ridge. Switchback three times to gain altitude.

Reach a junction. Keep left and contour along the slope. (To the right a side trail leads a short distance up to Kilo, a historic fish lookout.)

On the left pass Kapaʻeleʻele Koʻa, an ancient fish shrine.

Cross the rocky gully (map point C). On its far side reach another junction. Continue straight on a wide path through the forest. (To the left the improved trail parallels the gully initially and then eventually leads to the Kahana Valley State Park Visitors Center.)

Reach the edge of a ridge and turn right along it.

Climb gradually toward the Piei cliffs.

As the ridge narrows briefly, skirt to the right of an eroded section.

Keep to the left of a second eroded patch on the right side of the ridge.

Ascend gradually through grass and scattered trees on an indistinct trail. Generally, stay on the right side of the broad ridge and make your own trail, if necessary.

Cross a small eroded patch backed by hala trees.

As the ridge narrows, the trail becomes more distinct, and the vegetation increases.

Pass through hau trees and uluhe ferns.

The angle of ascent decreases briefly through a hala grove (phew!).

As the top nears, the ridge becomes more narrow and rocky.

Climb very steeply with the aid of two cables.

Reach the top of the Piei ridge (map point D) and turn left along it.

Climb over a small hump on a very narrow trail. There are cables on the worst sections.

Reach the broad summit of Pu'u Piei (elev. 1,740 ft) (map point E).

Notes

This hike gets down to business right away. It ascends 1,700 feet in a mile. That's serious climbing!

From the ridge top are great views of Kahana Bay and Valley in front and Punalu'u Valley in the rear. The prominent peak toward the back of Kahana Valley is Pu'u 'Ōhulehule. Behind it are the fluted cliffs of the Ko'olau summit.

Memorize the location of the first eroded section so you can key off of it on the way down.

Watch your footing on the narrow stretches. The ground there is often loose and crumbly. Test all cables before using them.

The trail receives sporadic maintenance, at best. The middle and upper sections overgrow between clearings.

38 Sacred Falls

Type:	Valley
Length:	5 mi round trip
Elev. Gain:	300 ft
Danger:	Low
Suitable for:	Novice
Location:	Windward Koʻolau Range above Hauʻula
Topo Map:	Hauʻula
Access:	Open

Trailhead Directions

At Punchbowl St. get on the Lunalilo Fwy (H-1) heading ʻewa (west).

Take Likelike Hwy (exit 20A, Rte 63 north) up Kalihi Valley through the Wilson Tunnel.

Turn left on Kahekili Hwy (Rte 83 west). That junction is the first major one after the tunnel and is marked Kahaluʻu—Lāʻie.

Kahekili Hwy becomes Kamehameha Hwy (still Rte 83), which continues up the windward coast.

Drive through the village of Kaʻaʻawa past the Crouching Lion Inn.

Go around Kahana Bay.

Pass Punaluʻu Beach Park on the right.

Pass Pat's at Punaluʻu on the right and the Greater Mt. Zion Holiness Church on the left.

Cross Kaluanui Stream on a bridge.

As a clear view of the ocean opens up on the right, turn left into Sacred Falls State Park.

Park in the large lot next to the main road (map point A).

Route Description

Cross the field in back of the parking lot.

Walk through an open gate and take the dirt road heading mauka.

Kaluanui Stream comes in on the left and parallels the road.

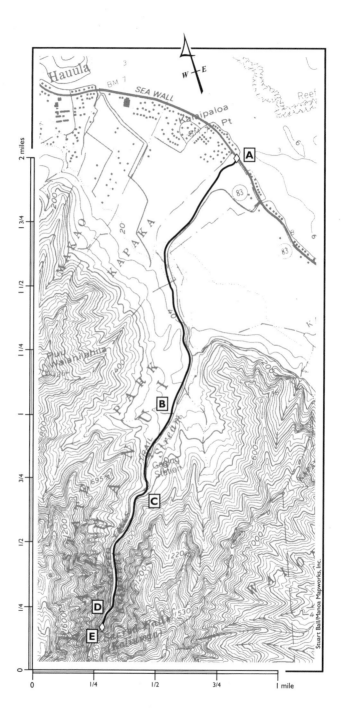

The road forks. Keep left on the dirt road. (To the right is a paved road with a chain across it.)

Cross a cattle grating.

The road ends at an open grassy area with several benches and palm trees (map point B).

The Sacred Falls Trail starts at the back of the open area.

Almost immediately cross an intermittent tributary of Kaluanui Stream.

Climb gradually along Kaluanui Stream under a canopy of Christmas berry trees. Some sections of the trail are rocky and rooty.

Go around to the right of a large boulder near the stream.

Cross the stream to its left side (map point C).

Pass three large mango trees on the right.

Go through a series of mountain apple groves.

The valley narrows to a gorge, and the trail becomes rougher.

Pass a smooth, rounded waterfall chute on the left.

Shortly afterward cross the stream on a jumble of rocks (map point D).

Climb the opposite bank and walk in the defile between the stream and the cliffs towering above.

Reach a good-sized pool (map point E). In back is powerful Kaliuwa'a (Sacred Falls).

Notes

Sacred Falls is popular with tourists and locals alike. The hike starts by the ocean, enters a wide valley, and ends in a gorge with a lovely pool and waterfall. In the last half mile the valley walls close in, and the expanse of sky above narrows to a ribbon.

The pool at the end is large enough for swimming. You can jump or dive off the low ledge on the right. Be sure to check the depth of the water first!

If it looks like it's raining hard up in the mountains, do not try the trail portion of this hike. The gorge is subject to severe flash flooding. If the water in the stream rises suddenly, move to high ground immediately. Wait there for the water to subside. Do not cross the stream if the water gets above your knees.

The trail receives regular maintenance and is usually clear. The footing is good, for the most part. However, be careful crossing the stream, because the rocks can be slippery.

There are some mosquitoes along the stream.

The mountain apples usually ripen in late July and early August.

According to legend, the waterfall chute near the falls was fashioned by the pig god Kamapua'a. He leaned against the cliff there so relatives could climb up his body and escape their enemies.

39 Hauʻula-Papali

Type:	Foothill
Length:	6 mi double loop
Elev. Gain:	700 ft (Hauʻula), 800 ft (Papali)
Danger:	Low
Suitable for:	Novice, Intermediate
Location:	Windward Koʻolau Range above Hauʻula
Topo Map:	Hauʻula
Access:	Open

Trailhead Directions

At Punchbowl St. get on the Lunalilo Fwy (H-1) heading ʻewa (west).

Take Likelike Hwy (exit 20A, Rte 63 north) up Kalihi Valley through the Wilson Tunnel.

Turn left on Kahekili Hwy (Rte 83 west). That junction is the first major one after the tunnel and is marked Kahaluʻu—Lāʻie.

Kahekili Hwy becomes Kamehameha Hwy (still Rte 83), which continues up the windward coast.

Drive through the villages of Kaʻaʻawa and Punaluʻu to Hauʻula.

Pass a fire station on the left.

Look for Hauʻula Beach Park on the right.

Park on Kamehameha Hwy at the far end of the beach park across from Hauʻula-Kahuku Congregational Church (map point A).

Route Description

Continue along Kamehameha Hwy on foot.

Turn left at the first intersection (Hauʻula Homestead Rd.).

As the paved road curves left, proceed straight on Maʻakua Rd. (dirt).

As the road curves slightly right, pass a private driveway on the left.

The road forks by a utility pole (map point B). Take the left fork.

Go around a chain across the road.

The road crosses a stream bed and curves right.

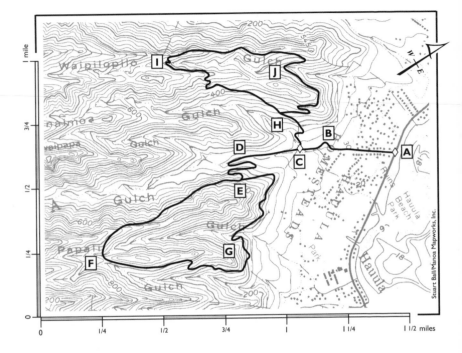

Reach a junction by a mango tree (map point C). Bear left, continuing on the dirt road. (To the right is the Hau'ula loop, which is described later on.)

After a short straightaway, reach a second junction (map point D). Bear left and down on the Papali-Ma'akua Ridge Trail. (To the right the road leads to the Ma'akua Gulch Trail.)

Almost immediately cross Ma'akua Stream and climb the embankment on the far side.

Work right and then left through a hau grove.

Climb gradually up the side of a ridge on eight switchbacks.

At the eighth one the trail splits, becoming a loop (map point E). Turn sharp right and start the loop in a counterclockwise direction.

Continue the ascent along the side of the ridge.

Reach the ridge line and climb gradually along it under an arch of trees.

Descend along the left side of the ridge into Papali Gulch.

Cross the stream there (map point F) and bear left downstream.

Climb gradually out of the gulch.

Gain the ridge line briefly near some Norfolk Island pines.

Switch to the right side of the ridge and descend gradually on a series of switchbacks.

Contour around the front of the ridge.

Descend once again into Papali Gulch and cross the rocky stream bed (map point G).

Climb out of the gulch on switchbacks.

Contour along the front of the next ridge.

Reach the end of the loop (map point E) and bear right and down.

Retrace your steps to the dirt road and its junction with the Hauʻula loop (map point C).

Turn left off the road onto the Hauʻula Loop Trail.

Follow Hānaimoa Stream briefly and then cross it.

Ascend through ironwoods on two switchbacks.

The trail splits, becoming a loop (map point H). This time keep left and start the loop in a clockwise direction.

Climb gradually up the side of a ridge on several switchbacks.

Reach the ridge line and cross over it.

Descend into Waipilopilo Gulch.

Cross the stream there (map point I) and climb out of the gulch.

Reach the ridge line and turn right, heading back toward the ocean.

Descend gradually, first along the top of the ridge, and then along its right side through a grove of Norfolk Island pines.

Drop into Waipilopilo Gulch once again (map point J) and then climb out of it.

Contour around the front of the ridge.

Reach the end of the loop (map point H) and turn left.

Retrace your steps back to the dirt road (map point C).

Turn left on it to return to the beach park (map point A).

Notes

The Hauʻula-Papali loops are perfect for beginning hikers. The route is obvious, and the trails are in good shape. The loops are not crowded, though, probably because of their distance from Honolulu.

The narrative follows the Papali loop first in a counterclockwise direction and then the Hauʻula loop in a clockwise direction. You can, of course, do just one or both loops in either order or direction. The Hauʻula loop is somewhat shorter and easier than Papali.

On the makai (ocean) section of the loops are good views of Hauʻula and Lāʻie towns.

The trails that make up the two loops receive regular maintenance and are thus usually clear. The footpath is, for the most part, wide and graded.

The Papali loop has banana liliko'i (passion fruit) on the ascending portion along the side of the ridge.

The first section of this hike on the dirt road is also part of the Ma'akua Gulch hike.

40 Maʻakua Gulch

Type:	Valley
Length:	6 mi round trip
Elev. Gain:	900 ft
Danger:	Low
Suitable for:	Intermediate
Location:	Windward Koʻolau Range above Hauʻula
Topo Map:	Hauʻula
Access:	Open

Trailhead Directions

At Punchbowl St. get on the Lunalilo Fwy (H-1) heading ʻewa (west).

Take Likelike Hwy (exit 20A, Rte 63 north) up Kalihi Valley through the Wilson Tunnel.

Turn left on Kahekili Hwy (Rte 83 west). That junction is the first major one after the tunnel and is marked Kahaluʻu—Lāʻie.

Kahekili Hwy becomes Kamehameha Hwy (still Rte 83), which continues up the windward coast.

Drive through the villages of Kaʻaʻawa and Punaluʻu to Hauʻula.

Pass the fire station on the left.

Look for Hauʻula Beach Park on the right.

Park on Kamehameha Hwy at the far end of the beach park across from Hauʻula-Kahuku Congregational Church (map point A).

Route Description

Continue along Kamehameha Hwy on foot.

Turn left at the first intersection (Hauʻula Homestead Rd.).

As the paved road curves left, proceed straight on Maʻakua Rd. (dirt).

As the road curves slightly right, pass a private driveway on the left.

The road forks by a utility pole (map point B). Take the left fork.

Go around a chain across the road.

The road crosses a stream bed and curves right.

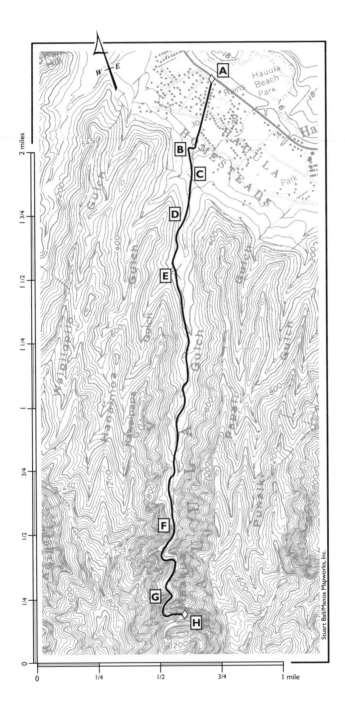

Reach a junction by a mango tree (map point C). Bear left, continuing on the dirt road. (To the right is the Hau'ula Loop Trail.)

After a short straightaway, reach a second junction (map point D). Keep right, on the road. (To the left is the Papali-Ma'akua Ridge Trail.)

Break out into the open and climb gradually above Ma'akua Stream.

The road ends at a turnaround. Continue straight on the Ma'akua Gulch Trail.

Descend briefly through hau.

In a grove of ironwoods cross Kawaipapa Stream, which comes in from the right (map point E).

Descend to Ma'akua Stream and cross it 13 times.

After the eleventh crossing the valley walls begin to close in.

At the thirteenth crossing a huge log spans the gulch (map point F). After that the stream becomes the trail more often than not.

As the stream twists and turns, pass several waterfall chutes, carved out of the near-vertical cliffs (map point G).

Reach a small pool where the gulch narrows to 5 feet across (map point H).

Swim through the pool to reach a second, larger one with a small waterfall. There the slippery cliffs block further progress upstream.

Notes

Ma'akua Gulch is the most spectacular of the valley hikes. The gulch is not very wide to begin with, and it gets very narrow very quickly. Toward the back the stream bends around towering rock dikes. The cliffs are scoured by near-vertical waterfall chutes. At the end you can touch the walls on either side with your outstretched arms.

July and early August are the best months to do this hike. The mountain apples are in season then. Also, the midday sun is high enough to reach the pool at the end of the hike. Without the sun the back of the gulch is a cold, damp hollow.

Much of the hike involves rock hopping in the stream. The rocks hopped upon are invariably the slippery ones. If possible, wear tabis (Japanese reef walkers) with a felt bottom. Hiking boots with a stiff sole are not recommended.

Ma'akua Stream is subject to flash flooding during very heavy rains. If the water rises above your knees, head for the nearest high ground and wait there for the stream to go down. It is far better to be stranded for half a day than to get swept away.

There are a lot of mosquitoes in the lower portion of the gulch.

The trail receives periodic maintenance. It overgrows slowly between clearings and so is usually open.

The Hau'ula-Papali hike starts from the same trailhead as this one. However, the two hikes are a world apart.

41 Koloa Gulch

Type:	Valley
Length:	8 mi round trip
Elev. Gain:	1,200 ft
Danger:	Low
Suitable for:	Novice, Intermediate
Location:	Windward Koʻolau Range above Lāʻie
Topo Map:	Kahuku, Hauʻula
Access:	Conditional; open to individuals and organized groups with written permission. Contact Zions Securities Corp., 55–510 Kamehameha Hwy, Lāʻie, HI 96762 (phone 293–9201).

Trailhead Directions

At Punchbowl St. get on the Lunalilo Fwy (H-1) heading ʻewa (west).

Take Likelike Hwy (exit 20A, Rte 63 north) up Kalihi Valley through the Wilson Tunnel.

Turn left on Kahekili Hwy (Rte 83 west). That junction is the first major one after the tunnel and is marked Kahaluʻu—Lāʻie.

Kahekili Hwy becomes Kamehameha Hwy (still Rte 83), which continues up the windward coast.

Drive through Kaʻaʻawa and Punaluʻu to Hauʻula.

Pass Hauʻula Beach Park on the right and Hauʻula Kai Shopping Center on the left.

Drive by a long rock wall on the right.

Park on the right shoulder of the highway next to the wooden fence of house number 55–135 (map point A). The house is 0.7 miles past the shopping center.

Route Description

Continue along Kamehameha Hwy on foot.

Cross a small culvert marked by yellow poles.

Almost immediately turn left on a dirt road across from house number 55–147.

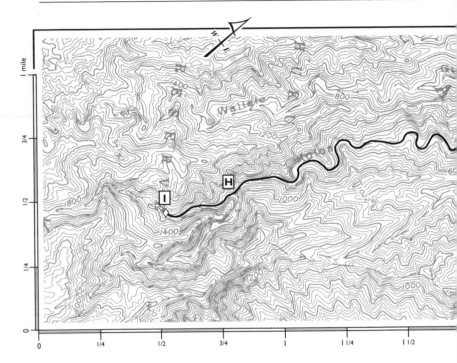

Take the first right by a farm house (map point B).

After passing a pump shack, the road forks (map point C). Take the left fork uphill.

The road forks again. Keep left. (The right fork leads to another house.)

The road turns sharp right along a row of ironwood trees.

Turn left on a grassy overgrown road by the last row of palm trees (map point D).

As the palms end, continue straight.

Descend through an opening in a fence by some Christmas berry trees.

Parallel a shallow gully on the right through scattered haole koa and Christmas berry.

Reach Koloa Stream and bear left upstream.

Climb over a large concrete irrigation pipe.

Begin climbing up the side of the ridge on the left.

Pass through an ironwood grove.

At a second grove reach the ridge line (map point E) and bear right uphill.

Ascend steadily through scattered ironwoods.

Descend briefly and then climb again across a narrow eroded section flanked by two scrawny ironwoods.

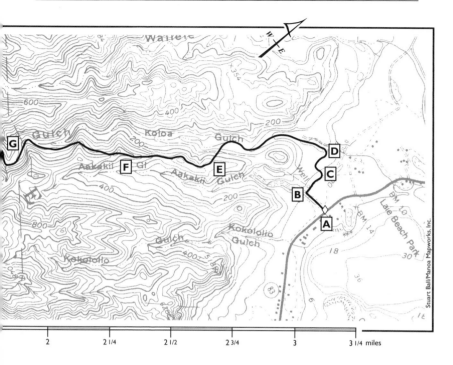

2   2 1/4   2 1/2   2 3/4   3   3 1/4 miles

Bear to the left to go around an eroded knob.

Just after a level grassy section reach a junction (map point F). Bear right off the ridge through a tunnel of guava. (The less-used trail to the left continues up the ridge.)

Descend back into the gulch, gradually at first, and then more steeply.

Reach Koloa Stream (map point G) and cross it. Bear left, heading upstream.

Cross the stream 22 more times. Highlights are as follows: After 4: a large stand of white ginger. After 8: a good camp site. At 9: the remains of a concrete dam. After 10: a grove of mango trees. At 15: twin stream beds with a tiny island in between.

After the twenty-third crossing, work around to the right of some huge boulders in the stream. Nestled among them is a small pool.

The trail becomes rough and obscure. Walk in the stream bed, as necessary.

The stream briefly splits and then rejoins. Keep to the right. Pass a small pool and a huge boulder on the right.

Reach a major fork in the stream (map point H). Again, keep to the right.

Pass two waterfall chutes as the gulch narrows significantly.

Reach a round, lovely pool backed by vertical cliffs and a small waterfall, which blocks further progress (map point I). Above and to the right is a larger waterfall.

Notes

Koloa Gulch penetrates into the heart of the windward Ko'olau Range. The hike starts in a wide, open valley and ends in a deep and narrow gulch. In the process you will cross Koloa Stream 23+ times. At the end is a small, but cool and refreshing pool for a dip. Novices can do the ridge section and then go as far as they want along the stream.

Some cautions are in order. The rocks in the stream are very, very slippery. Be conservative in your rock hopping! If possible, wear tabis (Japanese reef walkers) with felt bottoms. Also, Koloa Stream is subject to flash flooding during very heavy rains. If the water gets much above your knees, move to high ground and wait for the water to subside. Finally, there are a lot of mosquitoes in the lower section of the stream.

For a slightly longer hike, go left where the stream splits near the back of the gulch. Like the right, the left fork ends at a pool and a waterfall.

The ridge and stream trails receive periodic maintenance. They overgrow slowly between clearings and are thus usually open.

The ridge section has some strawberry guavas, and the stream section, some groves of mountain apple. The guavas usually ripen in August and September, and the apples, in July.

42 Lā'ie

Type:	Graded ridge
Length:	12 mi round trip
Elev. Gain:	2,200 ft
Danger:	Low
Suitable for:	Intermediate, Expert
Location:	Windward Ko'olau Range above Lā'ie
Topo Map:	Kahuku, Hau'ula
Access:	Conditional; open to individuals and organized groups with written permission. Contact Zions Securities Corp, 55-510 Kamehameha Hwy, Lā'ie, HI 96762 (phone 293-9201).

Trailhead Directions

At Punchbowl St. get on the Lunalilo Fwy (H-1) heading 'ewa (west).

Take Likelike Hwy (exit 20A, Rte 63 north) up Kalihi Valley through the Wilson Tunnel.

Turn left on Kahekili Hwy (Rte 83 west). That junction is the first major one after the tunnel and is marked Kahalu'u—Lā'ie.

Kahekili Hwy becomes Kamehameha Hwy (still Rte 83), which continues up the windward coast.

Drive through the villages of Ka'a'awa, Punalu'u, and Hau'ula to Lā'ie.

Pass the Polynesian Cultural Center and Lā'ie Shopping Center on the left.

Turn left on Naniloa Loop. That's the fourth left after the entrance road to the Mormon Temple. The loop has a grass median strip.

Enter a small traffic circle and exit at the second right on Po'ohaili St.

Park on the grass to the left by a baseball field (map point A).

Route Description

Continue along Po'ohaili St. on foot.

After passing the last house, go through a yellow gate.

Just past some guard rails the road becomes dirt.

Reach a fork. Keep left, past a utility pole.

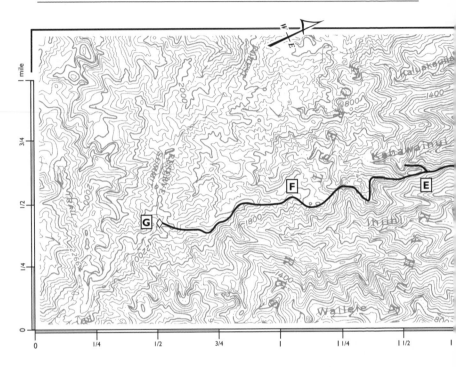

Shortly afterward the road forks again (map point B). This time keep right, following the line of utility poles.

Pass several aquaculture ponds and a pump shack on the right.

Reach a junction. Take the right fork across a small concrete bridge.

At the next junction turn left uphill (map point C).

At the next fork bear left, again uphill. (The right fork leads to an open dirt area.)

Another dirt road comes in on the left. Continue straight past some ironwoods.

At the next fork keep right, hugging the ridge.

Pass a barbed-wire fence extending left and right.

Curve right and then left on the road, now deeply rutted.

Reach another junction. Take the right, more eroded fork.

At an open, flat area keep right uphill on a very eroded section of the road.

The road narrows to a trail and is flanked by uluhe ferns and strawberry guavas.

Reach a grove of Norfolk Island pines (map point D). The Lā'ie Trail starts in the grove along the ridge line.

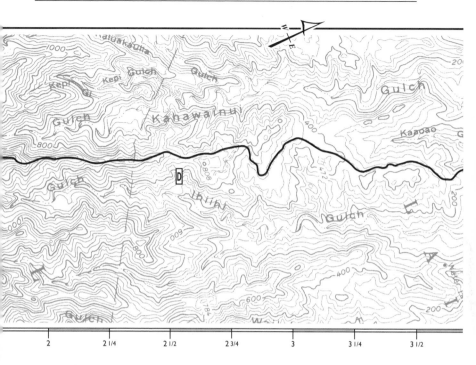

Descend briefly through the last of the pines.

Climb gradually along the left side of the ridge through a long stretch of strawberry guavas.

Right after the guavas switch to uluhe ferns, reach a junction (map point E). Keep left toward the summit. (To the right and up a low embankment is a short, but steep trail that leads down to a small pool and two waterfalls along Kahaiwainui Stream.)

Ascend gradually in and out of the small side gulches.

Pass an open stretch with a steep cliff on the right and sharp drop-off on the left.

Bear left and down into a gully to cross a large landslide blocking the original trail.

Climb out of the gully and continue the gradual ascent along the left side of the ridge.

Reach the ridge line and cross over to the right side of the ridge (map point F).

The gulch on the right narrows.

Work up the side of the gulch toward a small bowl in the summit ridge.

Pass a large Australian tea plant on the right.

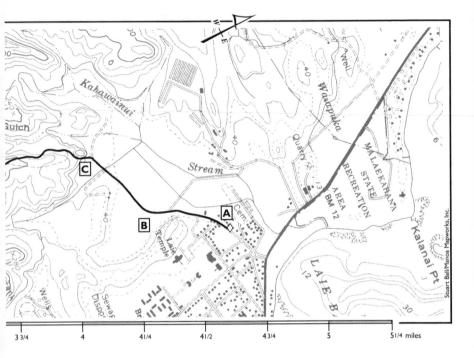

Just afterward cross the Ko'olau Summit Trail.

Climb the side of the bowl to reach the Ko'olau summit (elev. 2,240 ft) (map point G). The top is marked by a foxhole with a pole sticking out.

Notes

The Lā'ie hike is a study in contrasts. First comes a hot climb on a dry dirt road. Next follows an easy stroll through a cool corridor of Norfolk Island pines and strawberry guavas. Finally there is the rough wet slog through native forest to reach the summit.

From the top you can see Kahuku and Lā'ie towns to windward. The Wahiawā plain and the Wai'anae Range are to leeward. All around is the convoluted topography of the northern Ko'olau Range.

The pool on the side trail is small, but refreshing, especially after the hot climb on the road. Intermediate hikers can make the pool their goal. Summit hikers can wash their muddy boots and take a dip on the way back.

The Lā'ie Trail receives periodic maintenance. The upper and middle sections overgrow between clearings. The trail is almost always open as far as the pool.

Although basically graded, the trail above the pool has some uneven spots because of erosion and landslides. Watch your footing constantly. Expect to slip and fall and get muddy and wet.

The strawberry guavas along the lower section of the trail usually ripen in August and September.

The Koʻolau Summit Trail is a graded footpath that winds along the crest of the Koʻolau Range from the end of Pūpūkea Rd. to the end of the Kīpapa Ridge Trail. From the top of the Lāʻie Trail turn right to reach Pūpūkea Rd. Turn left to get to Kawailoa Ridge Trail and points south. Up Lāʻie, along the summit, and down Kawailoa makes a superb Koʻolau traverse. Remember that the Koʻolau Summit Trail is for experienced hikers only because it is overgrown, muddy, and sometimes narrow and obscure.

MAKAKILO TO MOKULĒ'IA

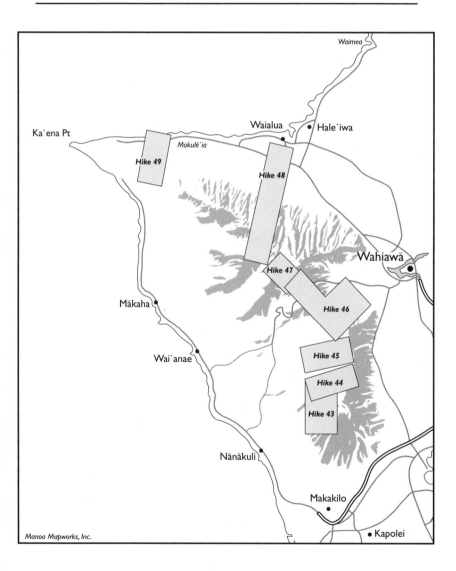

43 Pālehua

Type:	Foothill
Length:	9 mi loop
Elev. Gain:	1,500 ft
Danger:	Low
Suitable for:	Novice, Intermediate
Location:	Windward Wai'anae Range above Makakilo
Topo Map:	Schofield Barracks
Access:	Conditional; open only to outdoor clubs and organizations with permission. Call the Nature Conservancy (phone 537-4508).

Trailhead Directions

At Punchbowl St. get on the Lunalilo Fwy (H-1) heading 'ewa (west).

Near Middle St. keep left on Rte 78 west (exit 19B, Moanalua Rd.) to 'Aiea.

By Aloha Stadium bear right to rejoin H-1 to Pearl City and on toward Wai'anae.

Take exit 2, marked Barbers Pt NAS—Makakilo.

At the top of the off ramp turn right on Makakilo Dr.

Climb steadily through Makakilo.

Pass Makakilo Fire Station on the right and Makakilo Community Park on the left.

As the road curves right and down, turn left on Kīkaha St.

At the road end turn left on 'Umena St.

As 'Umena ends, continue straight on narrow, but paved Pālehua Rd.

Almost immediately reach a locked gate.

Contour through pasture land dotted with kiawe trees.

After curving right, the road splits. Take the right fork uphill. (The left fork, marked Timberline, continues to contour.)

Reach another locked gate at the forest reserve boundary.

Climb gradually through eucalyptus forest.

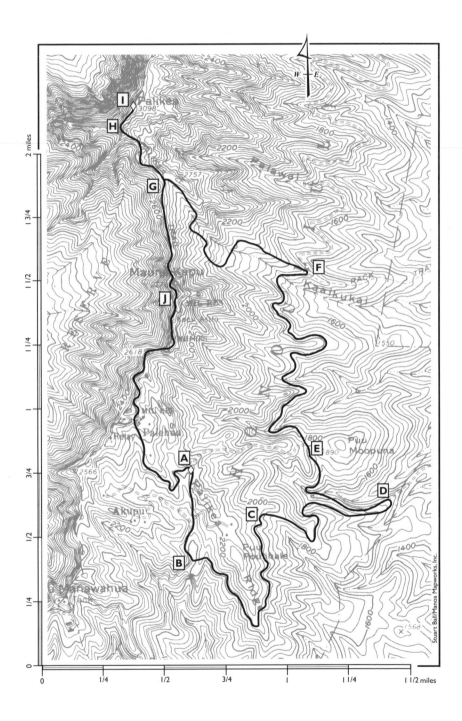

On the right look for the lower communications site, consisting of building no. 203 and two towers.

Park in front of the building (map point A).

Route Description

Walk back down Pālehua Rd.

Pass a dirt road on the left and another one on the right.

Just before reaching a small concrete culvert, turn left off the road on the Kupehau Trail (map point B).

At the top of the first side ridge, bear left and down into a narrow gulch.

Cross the gulch and descend alongside it.

Begin a long contour around Puʻu Poulihale.

Enter an evergreen forest of cedars and ironwoods.

Walk through several grassy areas with tall silk oaks.

Begin descending a ridge in back of Puʻu Poulihale (map point C).

As the ridge narrows, cross over its top to the right side.

Switchback to the left in a grove of ironwood trees.

Turn sharp right and back, bypassing an overgrown switchback.

Descend gradually just below and to the left of the ridge line.

The footway becomes less distinct through a grove of eucalyptus.

A dirt road comes in on the left (map point D). Turn sharp left on it.

Descend briefly to a small gulch and cross it.

Scramble through a tunnel of Christmas berry trees.

Climb gradually, paralleling the gulch on the left.

Swing right through heavy patches of grass.

Crawl over or under a series of fallen logs.

At the top of a side ridge reach an intersection with another dirt road (map point E). Continue straight across the intersection on a dirt road known as the Honouliuli Contour Trail. (The road to the left leads up to the lower communications site.)

Descend briefly and then begin contouring along the flank of the Waiʻanae Range.

Work into and out of six gulches. Highlights are as follows: After 1 is another Christmas berry tunnel. Just before 2 is a rock cliff on the left. 3 and 4 are smaller and less well defined. After 4 enter the Nature Conservancy's Honouliuli Preserve. 5 is covered with grass. 6 is Kaʻaikukui Gulch, which is lined with kukui trees.

Work out of the sixth gulch, passing a small double gulch.

Just before crossing the next side ridge, reach the junction with the Kaʻaikukui Gulch Trail in a grove of ironwoods (map point F). Turn sharp left and up on the gulch trail. (The contour trail continues straight and leads to the Palikea and Pu'u Kaua hikes.)

Climb gradually and cross a gully.

Curve right to parallel the gully.

Contour to the left and cross another gully.

Climb straight up.

Another gulch comes in on the left. Bear left to cross it.

Ascend steeply along the right side of that gulch.

Recross the gulch and continue to climb.

Work right to enter an ironwood grove.

Bear left and contour briefly on a well-defined road.

Cross a small gulch and at the next side ridge turn right uphill.

Turn right again to rejoin the road at a higher elevation.

Recross the gulch and enter the ironwoods again.

Cross another gulch.

Just after the third gulch, turn left, paralleling it.

Climb steeply. Drop into the gulch once to avoid a Christmas berry tangle.

Switchback once to gain elevation above the gulch.

Pass a dilapidated metal shack on the right.

Bear left and climb gradually to the Wai'anae summit.

There reach the junction with the Pālehua-Palikea Trail (map point G). Turn right on it. (To the left is the return portion of the loop.)

The trail splits. Take the left fork, which ascends a hill topped with Norfolk Island pines. (The right fork bypasses the hill.)

Descend the back side of the hill. The bypass trail comes in on the right.

Climb steeply up a second hill. A cable is provided for assistance in a particularly slippery spot.

Dip into a tiny notch and reach the top of a hill (map point H).

Turn right to continue along the summit ridge.

Reach Palikea (elev. 3,098 ft) (map point I). Its summit is marked by a group of ti plants.

Retrace your steps to the junction with the trail down Ka'aikukui Gulch (map point G). On the way back take the hill bypass trail to the left through a lovely grove of Norfolk Island pines.

Continue straight along the ridge through a flat grassy area.

Scramble under some large boulders.

Pass through an ironwood grove in a rocky section of the ridge.

Bear right to go around a large knob (Mauna Kapu).

Switchback twice up the side of the knob.

Enter a bamboo grove.

At the end of the grove turn left.

Pass two utility poles and a tower and then turn right down some steps.

Reach the upper communications site at the end of Pālehua Rd. (map point J).

Walk down Pālehua Rd. to the lower communications site (map point A).

Notes

Pālehua is a popular hike. It's not hard to see why. Your car does much of the climbing through the Wai'anae foothills. There are numerous options from very easy to fairly difficult. The route described is one of the longest but, as detailed below, is easily shortened. If you want to get your friends excited about hiking, take them on the magnificent ridge route to Palikea.

The views along the Wai'anae summit are superb. To leeward are Nānā-kuli and Lualualei Valleys. To windward are the Ko'olau Range, Pearl Harbor, and, in the distance, Honolulu and Diamond Head. To the north the Wai'anae Range culminates in the summit of Mt. Ka'ala.

There are several variations of this hike. For a shorter, 7-mile loop, elimi-nate the Kupehau section. Take the dirt road in back of building no. 203. At the first junction turn left on the Honouliuli Contour Trail and pick up the narrative from there. For an easy ridge hike, drive to the end of Pālehua Rd. Walk along the summit ridge to Palikea and come back the same way. The loops can, of course, be done in either direction.

The trails making up this hike receive sporadic maintenance. The ridge trail is usually open. The gulch and Kupehau trails overgrow slowly between clear-ings. Part of the contour trail overgrows quickly with grass. The Nature Con-servancy plans to open up the contour trail (and keep it open), so the grass may be a thing of the past.

The Honouliuli Contour Trail is a firebreak road that contours along the windward flank of the Wai'anae Range from Kolekole Pass to Pālehua Rd. In addition to Pālehua, the contour trail forms part of the Palikea, Pu'u Kaua, and Kānehoa-Hāpapa hikes.

The Palikea hike also climbs to the summit of Palikea but from the oppo-site direction.

44 Palikea

Type:	Ungraded ridge
Length:	8 mi round trip
Elev. Gain:	2,300 ft
Danger:	Low
Suitable for:	Intermediate, Expert
Location:	Windward Wai'anae Range above Village Park
Topo Map:	Schofield Barracks
Access:	Conditional; open to outdoor clubs and organizations with permission. Call Del Monte Corp. (phone 621–1201) and the Nature Conservancy (phone 537–4508).

Trailhead Directions

At Punchbowl St. get on the Lunalilo Fwy (H-1) heading 'ewa (west).

Near Middle St. keep left on Rte 78 west (exit 19B, Moanalua Rd.) to 'Aiea.

By Aloha Stadium bear right to rejoin H-1 to Pearl City and on toward Wai'anae.

Take Kunia Rd. (exit 5B, Rte 750 north).

Pass Village Park on the right and climb gradually through the cane fields.

Pass Garst Hawaii Research Center on the left.

Just afterward, cross Waiāhole ditch with its small reservoir on the right.

0.3 mi beyond the ditch, turn left into the pineapple fields on a dirt road.

Almost immediately cross a gully on a small rock causeway.

The road curves to the right and descends into a gulch.

Turn left and climb steeply out of the gulch.

Keep left along the edge of a pineapple field.

Go straight to avoid a small bulge in the field.

Park at the next bulge (map point A). Leave plenty of room for plantation vehicles to get by.

Route Description

Walk up to the next bulge in the field (map point B). There turn left on a dirt road overgrown with grass.

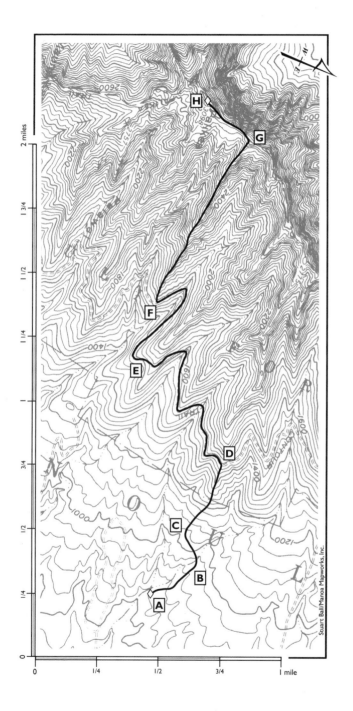

The road curves left and crosses a small gully.

As the road straightens out, look for a gate on the right (map point C). Climb over it into an overgrown pasture.

Ascend gradually toward the mountains. The trail varies from indistinct to nonexistent. Make your own, if necessary.

Go through a gate at the upper end of the pasture and enter the Nature Conservancy's Honouliuli Preserve.

Initially bear left and then continue straight up.

Reach the junction with the Honouliuli Contour Trail (map point D). It's marked by a white-barked tree. Turn left on the contour trail. (To the right the trail leads to the Pu'u Kaua and Kānehoa-Hāpapa hikes.)

Contour in and out of two gulches. The trail is heavily overgrown with grass in the sunny sections.

As the trail crosses the next side ridge, a dirt road comes in on the left (map point E). Keep right on the contour trail.

Pass an iron gate.

Work into and out of one more gulch.

As the contour trail crosses the next side ridge, turn right on a trail up that ridge (map point F). The initial section is up a very steep embankment. (The contour trail continues straight and leads to the Pālehua hike and Road.)

Climb steeply along the side ridge.

Reach the Wai'anae summit ridge (map point G). Turn left along it.

Descend briefly and then climb steeply. There is one cable for assistance.

Reach the summit of Palikea (elev. 3,098 ft) (map point H). Its top is marked by a group of ti plants.

Notes

The Pālehua hike is the easy way to get to the summit of Palikea. This hike is the hard way. Be prepared to wade through oceans of tall grass along the contour trail. Is this O'ahu or are we really in Africa? The hike does get better, though. The ridge section, although steep, is open and not too narrow. There are several interesting native plants along the way, including 'iliahi (sandalwood) and lapalapa. The lapalapa leaves flutter in the slightest wind.

From the top you can see Nānākuli and Lualualei Valleys to leeward. To windward are the Ko'olau Range, Pearl Harbor, and, in the distance, Honolulu and Diamond Head. To the north the Wai'anae Range continues to the summit of Mt. Ka'ala.

The trails making up this hike currently receive sporadic maintenance, at best. The contour trail overgrows quickly with tall grass between clearings. The ridge section overgrows more slowly. The Nature Conservancy plans to open up the contour trail (and keep it open), so the grass may be a thing of the past.

The Honouliuli Contour Trail is a firebreak road that contours along the windward flank of the Wai'anae Range from Kolekole Pass to Pālehua Rd. In addition to Palikea, the contour trail forms part of the Pu'u Kaua and Kāne-hoa-Hāpapa hikes.

The Pālehua hike also climbs to the summit of Palikea, but from the opposite direction.

45 Pu'u Kaua

Type:	Ungraded ridge
Length:	5 mi loop
Elev. Gain:	2,000 ft
Danger:	Medium
Suitable for:	Intermediate, Expert
Location:	Windward Wai'anae Range above Kunia
Topo Map:	Schofield Barracks
Access:	Conditional; open only to outdoor clubs and organizations with permission. Contact Del Monte Corp. (phone 621–1201) and the Nature Conservancy (phone 537–4508).

Trailhead Directions

At Punchbowl St. get on the Lunalilo Fwy (H-1) heading 'ewa (west).

Near Middle St. keep left on Rte 78 west (exit 19B, Moanalua Rd.) to 'Aiea.

By Aloha Stadium bear right to rejoin H-1 to Pearl City and on toward Wai'anae.

Take Kunia Rd. (exit 5B, Rte 750 north).

On the right pass Village Park subdivision.

Reach the Hawaii Country Club on the right.

Just past the clubhouse the road dips slightly and then climbs.

At the top of the rise and across from the boundary of the golf course, bear left on a dirt road paralleling the main highway.

By a raised water pipe turn left on a well-worn dirt road heading into the pineapple fields.

Curve right and then descend gradually to 'Ēkahanui Gulch.

Keep to the right of the gulch while ascending alongside it.

As the road tops out by some irrigation valves, turn left on a dirt road that descends briefly.

Climb gradually along the edge of a pineapple field. The gulch remains on the left.

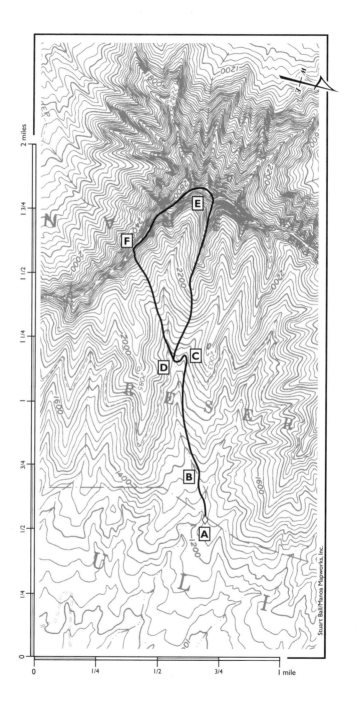

Park at the top of the field (map point A). Be sure to leave plenty of room for plantation vehicles to get by.

Route Description

As the road begins to curve right around the top of the pineapple field, bear left on a trail through the eucalyptus.

Descend gradually into 'Ēkahanui Gulch.

Cross a dry stream bed and turn left.

Work up, through a series of blowdowns left by hurricane 'Iwa.

Pick up an overgrown dirt road that curves right to contour along the flank of the mountain.

Bear left off the road to partially avoid another set of blowdowns.

Rejoin the road and cross a small stream bed (map point B). The road now becomes more open and defined.

Turn left straight uphill to bypass a clogged switchback on the road.

Turn left again to rejoin the road.

Climb steadily on the road, which becomes narrow and eroded.

As the road peters out, bear right up a short, steep section.

Reach the junction with the Honouliuli Contour Trail (map point C). Turn left on it. (To the right the contour trail leads to the Kānehoa-Hāpapa hike and Kolekole Pass.)

Descend briefly and cross a small stream bed (map point D). It marks the start and finish of the loop portion of this hike.

Leaving the contour trail, bear right and up on an indistinct trail.

Climb steeply on the broad ridge through guava. The going is mostly straight up with an occasional attempt at a switchback.

The ridge narrows, and the incline lessens briefly.

Resume the steep ascent on the now partially open ridge.

Negotiate a particularly steep, wet section through native vegetation.

Reach the top of Pu'u Kaua (elev. 3,127 ft) in a grassy area (map point E).

Turn left along the summit ridge of the Wai'anae Range.

Cross the broad top of Kaua.

Descend steeply on the open, narrow ridge dotted with Christmas berry.

Go left around a rock face.

Traverse a relatively level section and climb a tiny hump.

About 30 yd past the hump, turn left straight down the flank of the summit ridge (map point F). There is no distinct side ridge at the turnoff.

Descend very steeply.

Halfway down pick up a distinct side ridge. The angle of descent gradually decreases.

Go through a forest of large silk oaks and guava on a faint trail.
Enter a grassy section with some guava.
Walk across some small broken-up logs.
About 30 yd beyond, bear left off the side ridge.
Descend steeply into the gully on the left.
Cross the stream bed and turn right downstream.
The trail gradually climbs out of the gully and then parallels it.
Descend along the left side of a small ridge.
Bear left and down to the original dry stream bed (map point D). There the loop ends.
Retrace your steps back to the trailhead (map point A).

Notes

Pu'u Kaua is O'ahu's third highest peak. The climb to the summit is not particularly difficult, although there are some steep sections. The hike is a loop and thus includes a short, marvelous stretch along the Wai'anae summit. The descent is along a very steep, forested side ridge.

From the top you can see Lualualei and Wai'anae Valleys to leeward. To windward are the north shore, the Wahiawā plain, and the Ko'olau Range. To the north along the summit ridge are Kolekole Pass and Mt. Ka'ala.

The initial trail section is somewhat obscure, with lots of twists and turns. Follow the route description closely. There may be ribbons marking the way but don't count on it.

The trail receives periodic maintenance. It overgrows slowly between clearings and so is usually open.

During a heavy rain the pineapple road quickly becomes impassable for regular cars. If the road is muddy and slippery, leave your car by Kunia Rd. or park by the irrigation valves before the road dips.

The Honouliuli Contour Trail is a firebreak road that contours along the windward flank of the Wai'anae Range from Kolekole Pass to Pālehua Rd. In addition to Pu'u Kaua, the contour trail forms part of the Pālehua, Palikea, and Kānehoa-Hāpapa hikes.

46 Kānehoa-Hāpapa

Type:	Ungraded ridge
Length:	5 mi one way
Elev. Gain:	1,900 ft
Danger:	Medium
Suitable for:	Intermediate, Expert
Location:	Windward Wai'anae Range above Kunia
Topo Map:	Schofield Barracks
Access:	Conditional; open only to outdoor clubs and organizations with permission. Contact Del Monte Corp. (phone 621–1201), the Nature Conservancy (phone 537–4508), and the Directorate of Facilities Engineering, U.S. Army Support Command, Fort Shafter, HI 96858.

Trailhead Directions

The directions, as given, assume you are doing the hike one way and have two cars.

At Punchbowl St. get on the Lunalilo Fwy (H-1) heading 'ewa (west).

Near Middle St. keep left on Rte 78 west (exit 19B, Moanalua Rd.) to 'Aiea.

By Aloha Stadium bear right to rejoin H-1 to Pearl City.

Take the H-2 freeway (exit 8A) to Wahiawā.

As the freeway ends, continue on Rte 99 north (Wilikina Dr.) bypassing Wahiawā.

At the first traffic light turn left on Kunia Rd.

At the next light turn right and enter Schofield Barracks through the Foote Gate.

Bear right on Devol Rd.

At the road end turn left on Wai'anae Ave., which is one way.

Turn left on Glennan Rd. as Wai'anae Ave. splits.

At the road end turn right on Trimble Rd. by the commissary.

Trimble Rd. narrows to two lanes and becomes Kolekole Rd.

Ascend gradually toward Kolekole Pass.

Go through a series of S curves.

Look for a large sign on the left marked Kolekole Pass Rock. It's just before the guard station at the top of the pass.

Park one car in the dirt lot next to the sign (map point K).

In the second car exit Schofield Barracks through the Foote Gate and turn right on Kunia Rd.

The road narrows to two lanes and dips.

Pass Kunia Field Station on the right.

On the right look for a pineapple staging area with stacked frames. In back and to the right is a red-and-white radar tower.

Just before the frames, turn right into the pineapple fields.

Take the main dirt road heading toward the mountains.

Pass a black-and-white tank and the red-and-white tower on the right.

A power line joins the road and parallels it.

Take the last left before the road dips into a gulch. That turn is marked by an old water pipe in the middle of the intersection.

Climb gradually on the well-worn road, which is bordered on the left by a grassy strip.

On the right at the top of a rise, look for a grassy mound surrounded by a barbed-wire fence. The mound is the side of a reservoir, but the water is not visible from below.

Park there along the main road (map point A). Leave plenty of room for plantation vehicles to get by. Behind and to the right of the reservoir is a large green backboard, which can be seen just after the turnoff from Kunia Rd.

Route Description

Walk up the dirt road heading toward the backboard.

Work left and then right to arrive at its base. The trail starts just to the left of the backboard.

Ascend next to a small gully of red dirt.

Reach the ridge line (map point B) and bear left, up through a eucalyptus forest.

Enter the Nature Conservancy's Honouliuli Preserve.

Reach the top of Mauna Una hill (map point C). It's marked by a benchmark on the left and a triangulation station platform on the right.

In a grove of evergreens reach the junction with the Honouliuli Contour Trail (map point D). Continue straight up the ridge. (To the right the contour trail goes to Kolekole Pass. To the left the trail leads to the Pu'u Kaua, Palikea, and Pālehua hikes.)

Ascend, steeply at first, and then more gradually.

Descend briefly and then begin a long gradual climb to the top.

Reach the Wai'anae summit at an eroded spot (map point E). The knob just to the left is Pu'u Kānehoa (elev. 2,778 ft).

Turn right along the summit ridge.

Traverse a rocky, narrow section. Go around to the left of the worst spot.

Climb over a knob in the ridge.

Bear left and down to avoid two large rock formations.

Ascend a second knob and drop steeply off its back side.

Bypass the top of a third, rocky knob that juts out from the ridge.

Ascend gradually over a series of much smaller humps.

The vegetation opens up on the approach to Pu'u Hāpapa.

Dip slightly through a grove of Christmas berry.

Climb a small rock face. A cable is provided for assistance.

Ascend steeply to the summit of Hāpapa (elev. 2,883 ft) (map point F) and cross its broad top.

Leave the Honouliuli Preserve.

After passing a small eroded area, reach a junction. Continue along the

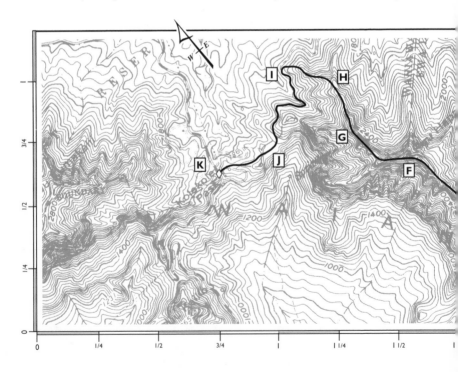

2	2 1/4	2 1/2	2 3/4	3	3 1/4 miles

main ridge toward Kolekole Pass. (The trail to the right leads down a side ridge to the Honouliuli Contour Trail.)

Reach a second junction marked by a lichen-covered rock in a stand of Christmas berry trees. Bear right. (The trail to the left ends in a sheer precipice!)

Descend along the rocky, open ridge.

Pass a faint trail leading down the first side ridge on the left (map point G). Continue along the main ridge.

Reach another junction just past a small stand of koa and silk oaks (map point H). Turn left down the open side ridge.

As the ridge widens, the trail splits. Keep left again.

Descend steeply on a narrow, rocky trail.

Reach the Honouliuli Contour Trail (map point I). Turn left on it by an overhanging Christmas berry tree.

Cross a rocky stream bed.

Walk through a large grove of paperbark trees.

Cross a small slide on a skinny trail.

Break out into the open by an eroded hill.

Enter a lovely small meadow (map point J).

Pick up a dirt road on the far side of the meadow.

Descend toward Kolekole Pass. A road comes in on the right and then one on the left.

Reach a more traveled dirt road. Bear right on it, passing a tower on the left.

To the right walk up some steps leading to Kolekole Pass Rock.

Take the path behind the rock.

Descend on wooden steps.

Reach the dirt parking lot on Kolekole Rd (map point K).

Notes

This hike traverses a long section of the scenic Wai'anae summit ridge. In the process you pass one peak, Kānehoa, climb another, Hāpapa, and then descend precipitously to Kolekole Pass. Kānehoa-Hāpapa is a favorite with local hikers because the ridge walking is spectacular without becoming too dangerous or exhausting.

The views all along the summit are breathtaking. To leeward are Lualualei and Wai'anae Valleys. To windward are the Wahiawā plain, Pearl Harbor, and, in the distance, Honolulu and Diamond Head. In back you can see the Ko'olau Range from the north shore to Nu'uanu Pali.

Be careful on the rocky, narrow section just past Kānehoa. Be sure of your footing in the grassy stretches along the summit. The grass can hide steep drop-offs in the ridge. Test the cable on the rock face before using it. There are numerous variations of this hike. As described, the route is one way from the pineapple fields to Kolekole Pass and requires two cars. You can, of course, do the hike in the opposite direction. If you just have one car, start from either trailhead and walk as far as you like. Remember to get the correct permits, though. If you go through the pineapple fields, you must contact Del Monte. If you start from Kolekole Pass, you must contact the Army. You must always check with the Nature Conservancy because all possible routes go through their Honouliuli Preserve.

There is one more variation for experienced hikers only. Use the Honouliuli Contour Trail to make a loop. From Hāpapa take the trail down the side ridge. Turn right on the contour trail. Turn left by the evergreens and retrace your steps to the pineapple fields. The route is obscure and overgrown, to say the least. The Nature Conservancy plans to open up the contour trail (and keep it open), so this variation may be less difficult in the near future.

The trails on this hike receive periodic maintenance. They overgrow slowly between clearings and so are usually open.

The Honouliuli Contour Trail is a firebreak road that contours along the windward flank of the Wai'anae Range from Kolekole Pass to Pālehua Rd. In addition to Kānehoa-Hāpapa, the contour trail forms part of the Pu'u Kaua, Palikea, and Pālehua hikes.

The Pu'u Kalena hike starts on the opposite side of Kolekole Pass.

47 Pu'u Kalena

Type:	Ungraded ridge
Length:	5 mi round trip
Elev. Gain:	1,900 ft
Danger:	High
Suitable For:	Expert
Location:	Windward Wai'anae Range above Schofield Barracks
Topo Map:	Schofield Barracks
Access:	Conditional; open to individuals and organized groups with written permission. Write the Directorate of Facilities Engineering, U.S. Army Support Command, Fort Shafter, HI 96858.

Trailhead Directions

At Punchbowl St. get on the Lunalilo Fwy (H-1) heading 'ewa (west).

Near Middle St. keep left on Rte 78 west (exit 19B, Moanalua Rd.) to 'Aiea.

By Aloha Stadium bear right to rejoin H-1 to Pearl City.

Take the H-2 freeway (exit 8A) to Wahiawā.

As the freeway ends, continue on Rte 99 north (Wilikina Dr.) bypassing Wahiawā.

At the first traffic light turn left on Kunia Rd.

At the next light turn right and enter Schofield Barracks through the Foote Gate.

Bear right on Devol Rd.

At the road end turn left on Wai'anae Ave., which is one way.

Turn left on Glennan Rd. as Wai'anae Ave. splits.

At the road end turn right on Trimble Rd. by the commissary.

Trimble Rd. narrows to two lanes and becomes Kolekole Rd.

Ascend gradually toward Kolekole Pass.

Go through a series of S curves.

Watch for a yellow sign indicating heavy equipment crossing.

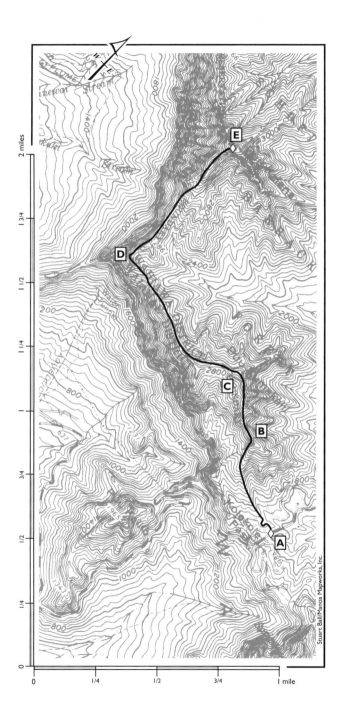

Just after the sign a gravel road marked Rock Quarry comes in on the right.

Park in the grassy lot on the left across from the gravel road (map point A).

Route Description

Walk back down Kolekole Rd.

About 25 yd past the gravel road, turn left into the forest on a trail.

Climb straight up briefly and then bear left on an overgrown dirt road.

Bear right and up off the road to shortcut a switchback.

Regain the road and switchback four times.

Pass a metal stake in the ground and switchback to the right.

Switchback left and in 30 yards reach a junction. Turn right and up on a trail. (The road, which has been recently bulldozed, continues its gradual ascent.)

Climb very steeply along the edge of a ridge. There are two cables for assistance.

Reach a rocky outcrop with a benchmark (map point B).

The ridge levels momentarily.

Resume steep climbing over rock.

Bypass a narrow section to the left.

The ridge again levels briefly.

Climb gradually on a narrow rock dike.

Ascend more steeply, negotiating a small rock face.

Reach the top of Pu'u Kū Makali'i (map point C).

Bear left to continue along the main ridge.

The next section is relatively level, but quite narrow.

Descend gradually along the ridge through a lovely forest of 'ōhi'a and introduced species.

Go around to the right of a large slide.

Reach a flat area. Keep left there, continuing along the main ridge.

Descend steeply to a saddle.

Ascend a small dirt hump in the middle of the saddle.

Climb steeply on the eroded trail to reach a distinct peak (map point D).

At its top turn right, again following the main ridge.

Descend into a second saddle and ascend to another smaller peak.

Descend steeply and then begin the final climb to the summit of Kalena.

Climb very steeply through uluhe ferns.

Reach a relatively level section.

Resume climbing through native rain forest.

Reach the summit of Pu'u Kalena (elev. 3,504 ft) (map point E).

Notes

Kalena is the second highest peak on O'ahu. The ascent to its summit is short, steep, and a bit scary, but absolutely superb. Serious climbing starts right away, so the hike is for experts only. The views all along the hike are panoramic. To leeward are Lualualei and Wai'anae valleys. To windward are the north shore, the Wahiawā plain, and, in the distance, Honolulu and Diamond Head. In back is the Ko'olau Range. To the north, along the Wai'anae summit ridge, is massive Mt. Ka'ala. To the south are Kolekole Pass and the peaks of Hāpapa, Kānehoa, and Kaua.

Remember to keep left after passing the benchmark on the way back. There are several indistinct trails on the right that could be mistaken for the main route.

The dike sections on this hike are very narrow and often have drop-offs on both sides. Use extreme caution. If necessary, crawl along the top. It's not elegant, but it's a whole lot safer.

The trail receives periodic maintenance. The blackberry bushes on the final climb overgrow between clearings. Wear gloves and long pants for protection against the thorns. The remainder of the hike is usually open.

The Kānehoa-Hāpapa hike finishes on the opposite side of Kolekole Pass.

48 Dupont

Type:	Ungraded ridge
Length:	11 mi round trip
Elev. Gain:	4,000 ft
Danger:	Medium
Suitable for:	Intermediate, Expert
Location:	Windward Wai'anae Range above Waialua
Topo Map:	Hale'iwa
Access:	Conditional; open to individuals and organized groups with written permission. Contact Waialua Sugar Co. (phone 637–3521), Waialua Ranch (phone 637–9441), and Kamananui Orchard (phone 637–4834).

Trailhead Directions

At Punchbowl St. get on the Lunalilo Fwy (H-1) heading 'ewa (west).

Near Middle St. keep left on Rte 78 west (exit 19B, Moanalua Rd.) to 'Aiea.

By Aloha Stadium bear right to rejoin H-1 to Pearl City.

Take the H-2 freeway (exit 8A) to Wahiawā.

As the freeway ends, continue on Rte 99 north (Wilikina Dr.) bypassing Wahiawā.

Pass Schofield Barracks on the left.

The road narrows to two lanes, dips, and then forks. Take the left fork toward Waialua (still Wilikina Dr., but now Rte 803).

Wilikina Dr. becomes Kaukonahua Rd. (still Rte 803).

At Thomson Corner (flashing yellow light) continue straight on Farrington Hwy (Rte 930).

At the small traffic circle bear left under the overpass to Mokulē'ia.

Look for Waialua High School on the left.

Park on the street next to the school's last lot (map point A).

Route Description

Continue along Farrington Hwy toward Mokulē'ia on foot.

Just past the high school turn left on a semipaved cane road (map point B).

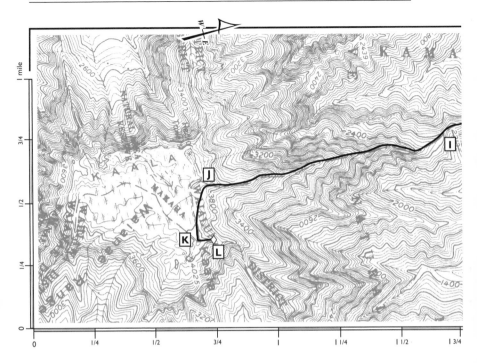

Climb over a locked yellow gate.

Pass the high school football field on the left.

Near the end of the cane fields pass a small reservoir on the left (map point C).

Go through a white gate.

The road, now dirt, bears right and begins to climb.

Another dirt road comes in on the right. Keep left.

As the road curves right, bear left through a wooden gate (map point D). Use the ladder on the left side.

Follow a grassy road through the pasture. Initially, the road bears left and then works right, past a watering trough.

Climb steadily to reach the crest of a broad ridge.

Bear left up the ridge, still on the road (map point E).

Pass a large bare spot.

The road becomes indistinct in several places. Keep to the ridge line.

Pass another watering trough on the right in a large eroded area.

Continue climbing through patches of trees as the road becomes more obscure.

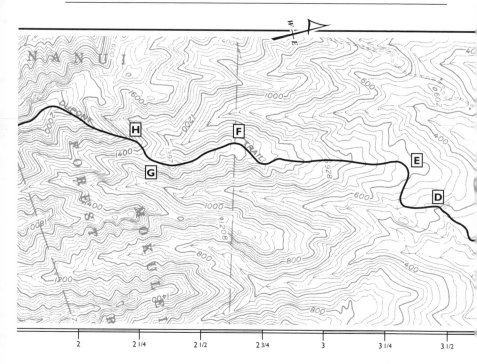

Reach the Mokuleʻia Forest Reserve boundary marked by an old wood-and-wire fence at the road end (map point F). Use the built-in steps to climb over the broken-down gate.

Traverse a pleasant level section through mixed dry-land vegetation.

Descend briefly to a wooded saddle (map point G).

Climb very steeply on the severely eroded trail.

Reach the main ridge line (map point H) and bear left through strawberry guavas.

Climb steeply past an eroded area with a panoramic view.

The angle of ascent eases through another pleasant section of dry-land forest.

Begin serious climbing as the ridge narrows and becomes rocky.

Cross a narrow eroded neck (map point I).

Reach a 30-ft drop in the ridge. Descend it with the help of a cable.

Negotiate several steep, narrow spots with bad footing. Again, cables are provided.

Continue the steep, slippery climb, now through native forest with some blackberry bushes.

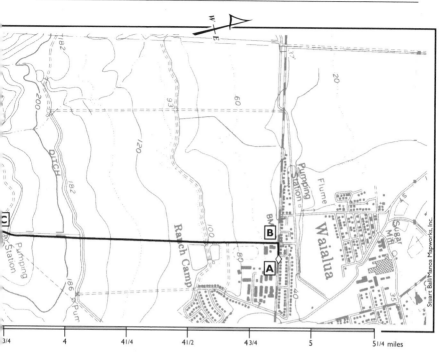

Pass a small shack with two radars nearby.

The trail becomes a stairway with handrails.

On the right pass another shack with antennas.

Bear left and cross a small green wooden bridge.

Reach the paved Mt. Kaʻala Rd. at a convex, blind-spot mirror (map point J). Turn left on the road.

Another paved road comes in on the right. Keep left on the main road.

Reach the summit of Mt. Kaʻala (elev. 4,025 ft) (map point K) near the main gate of an FAA radar installation.

Turn left off the road by a yellow reflector. Just past the small tower on the right is a good view point (map point L).

Notes

If Castle is the classic climb in the Koʻolau Range, Dupont is its counterpart in the Waiʻanae Range. The trail ascends Mt. Kaʻala, Oʻahu's highest peak, from the windward side. On the way up you pass through cane fields, cattle pasture, dry-land forest, and rain forest. On the summit plateau is a cool, misty bog with an incredibly rich variety of native plants.

From the view point on top you can see all of the north shore and the towns of Waialua and Hale'iwa. The Wahiawā plain and Ko'olau Range are in the distance to the right. If the view is obscured, wait a while. The mist comes and goes.

Do not enter the FAA radar installation, even though the main gate is sometimes open. They don't welcome tourists!

To visit the bog, turn right near the FAA main gate and cross a flat grassy helipad. Look for a low fence with a gate. Go through the unlocked gate and follow a boardwalk. It leads across the bog to the leeward side of the summit plateau. Stay on the boardwalk to avoid damaging the vegetation.

The walk across the bog is also part of the Wai'anae Ka'ala hike. Up Dupont and down Wai'anae Ka'ala makes a superb traverse of the mountain.

There have been numerous horror stories written and told about the Dupont Trail. It is nowhere near as difficult or scary as the stories would have you believe. Nevertheless, the hike is not a cakewalk. The climbing is constant and sometimes very steep. Watch your footing and balance on the narrow slippery sections. Test all cables before using them. Intermediates can go as far as they feel comfortable and then turn around.

The Dupont Trail receives periodic maintenance. The lower and middle sections overgrow slowly between clearings and so are usually open. The upper section has some blackberry patches, which grow fast. Wear gloves and long pants for protection against the thorns.

The Mt. Ka'ala Rd. leads down to Farrington Hwy on the Mokulē'ia side. The road is not a good exit because it is long, boring, hard on the feet and knees, and closed to the public.

49 Keālia

Type:	Graded ridge
Length:	7 mi round trip
Elev. Gain:	1,900 ft
Danger:	Low
Suitable for:	Intermediate
Location:	Windward Wai'anae Range above Mokulē'ia
Topo Map:	Ka'ena
Access:	Open

Trailhead Directions

At Punchbowl St. get on the Lunalilo Fwy (H-1) heading 'ewa (west).

Near Middle St. keep left on Rte 78 west (exit 19B, Moanalua Rd.) to 'Aiea.

By Aloha Stadium bear right to rejoin H-1 to Pearl City.

Take the H-2 freeway (exit 8A) to Wahiawā.

As the freeway ends, continue on Rte 99 north (Wilikina Dr.) bypassing Wahiawā.

Pass Schofield Barracks on the left.

The road narrows to two lanes, dips, and then forks. Take the left fork toward Waialua (still Wilikina Dr., but now Rte 803).

Wilikina Dr. becomes Kaukonahua Rd. (still Rte 803).

At Thomson Corner (flashing yellow light) continue straight on Farrington Hwy (Rte 930).

At the small traffic circle bear left under the overpass to Mokulē'ia.

Pass Waialua High School on the left.

Drive through Mokulē'ia.

On the left pass Dillingham Air Field and Glider Port, surrounded by a green fence.

At the far end of the runway turn left through a break in the fence by a red airfield sign.

Go around the end of the runway and head back along the other side.

Pass a low concrete building on the left.

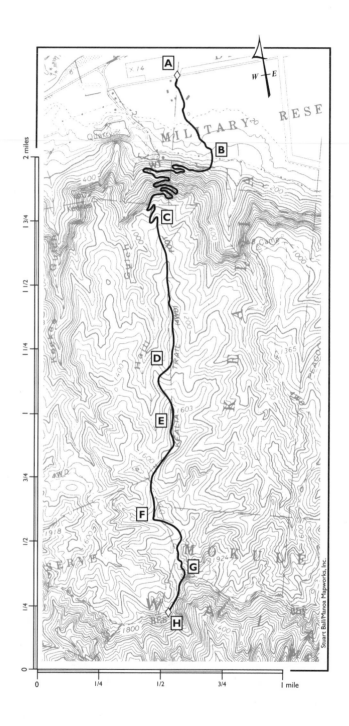

Turn right by a speed limit sign on a broad paved road.

Park off the road on the right across from a hose and a no vehicle washing sign (map point A).

Route Description

Just past the hose, bear left. Keep a large concrete building on your right.

The road narrows to a gravel track.

Another road comes in on the left. Keep right.

Reach a low green fence with an unlocked gate (map point B).

Go through the gate and immediately bear left on the Keālia Trail.

Work toward the base of the cliffs through grass and haole koa.

The trail splits. Take the right fork.

Ascend the pali gradually on 14 switchbacks.

Reach the top of the cliff at an ironwood grove (map point C).

Follow a tiny gully through the grove.

Climb gradually up the wide ridge through grass dotted with silk oaks and Christmas berry.

Bear right through tall grass just before reaching an old fence and gate.

Descend briefly on a dirt road overgrown with grass.

The road opens up and begins to contour along the side of the ridge.

Swing right to cross a gulch and then climb through a stand of ironwoods.

Just before the road descends, turn left and up on an eroded dirt road (map point D).

Climb steeply through eucalyptus.

Pass an open bare area with good views of the north shore (map point E).

The road ends at a T junction. Turn left on another dirt road and climb steeply.

A road comes in on the right. Continue straight and up.

A road comes in on the left. Keep right and up.

Descend steeply and then ascend.

The road ends at another T junction (map point F). Turn left on the Mokulē'ia firebreak road toward Mākua Valley. (To the right the firebreak road leads to the Ka'ena Point Satellite Tracking Station.)

Reach a four-way junction. Continue straight and up on a less-traveled road. (The Mokulē'ia firebreak road veers left.)

Reach a junction at the road end (elev. 1,960 ft) (map point G). Turn right and down on a trail along the edge of Mākua Valley. (To the left a trail leads to the Mokulē'ia firebreak road and the Mākua Rim Trail.)

Reach an overlook with rock slabs (map point H).

Notes

Keālia starts with an exhilarating climb of the pali behind Dillingham Air Field. Unfortunately, the middle portion of the hike involves a lot of tedious road walking. The finish, however, at an overlook of Mākua Valley is well worth the effort.

From the upper switchbacks are great views of Waialua and Hale'iwa towns and the north shore. The Ko'olau Range is in the distance beyond the cane fields. Watch for the fixed-wing gliders soaring above the air field. From the overlook at the end of the hike you can see expansive Mākua Valley and the Wai'anae Range all the way to Mt. Ka'ala.

The best time to do this hike is February to April. The weather is cooler then, and you'll miss the pig and bird hunting seasons.

Do not descend into Mākua Valley. It is a military range used for live fire exercises.

The Keālia Trail receives periodic maintenance. The stretch below the pali and on the switchbacks overgrows slowly between clearings. Most of the trail is graded, and the footing is good.

The sections of this hike along the firebreak road and on the trail to the overlook are also part of the Kuaokalā hike.

The Mokulē'ia firebreak road follows the crest of the Wai'anae Range toward an abandoned Nike missile site. Before reaching it, the road contours around the site and connects with its paved access road. The Mākua Rim Trail starts in back of the Nike site and follows the edge of Mākua Valley. The trail leads to a good campsite near the Pahole Natural Area Reserve. See the Kuaokalā hike for a brief description of a great 2- to 3-day camping trip in this area.

Leeward Wai'anae Range

WAI'ANAE TO KA'ENA POINT

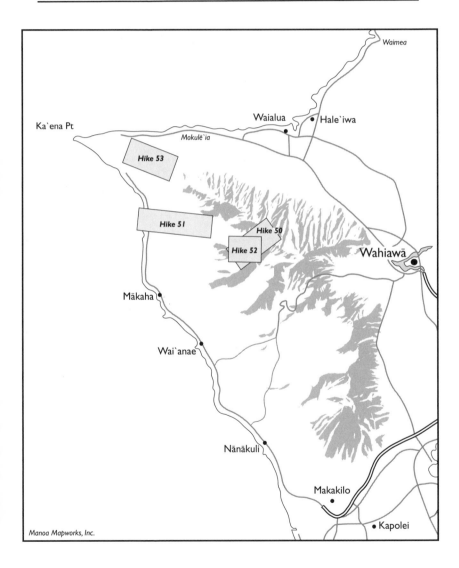

50 Wai'anae Ka'ala

Type:	Ungraded ridge
Length:	5 mi round trip
Elev. Gain:	2,600 ft
Danger:	Medium
Suitable for:	Intermediate, Expert
Location:	Leeward Wai'anae Range above Wai'anae town
Topo Map:	Wai'anae, Ka'ena, Hale'iwa
Access:	Open

Trailhead Directions

At Punchbowl St. get on the Lunalilo Fwy (H-1) heading 'ewa (west).

Near Middle St. keep left on Rte 78 west (exit 19B, Moanalua Rd.) to 'Aiea.

By Aloha Stadium bear right to rejoin H-1 to Pearl City and on toward Wai'anae.

As the freeway ends near Campbell Industrial Park, continue along the leeward coast on Farrington Hwy (Rte 93).

Drive through Nānākuli and Mā'ili to Wai'anae town.

After passing Burger King on the right, begin counting traffic lights. At the third one, by Wai'anae Coast Drive-In, turn right on Wai'anae Valley Rd.

Reach a bus turnaround marked with white curbs.

Take the one-lane paved road to the left at the back of the circle.

The pavement disappears briefly by some houses and then resumes.

Keep left on the paved road at two junctions. The last one is marked with a large Wai'anae Kai Forest Reserve sign.

Climb steadily through open country.

Pass a water tank on the left.

In a forested area the road levels off momentarily and passes between two concrete buildings surrounded by chain-link fences.

Ascend steeply through the forest.

Reach two concrete buildings and the end of the paved road.

Park on the right off the road near the buildings (map point A).

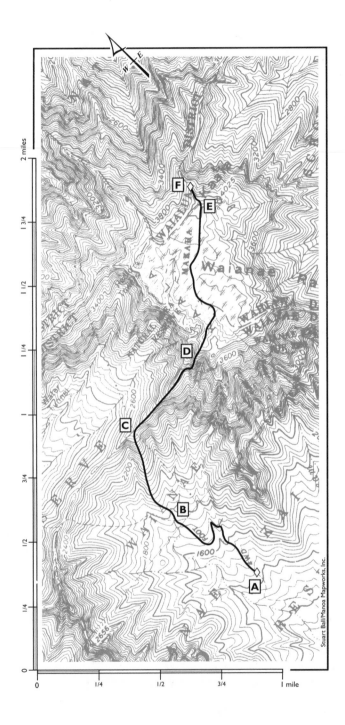

Route Description

Continue up the road (now dirt) to its end at a turnaround loop.

On the right of the loop take the trail marked by four boulders.

Ascend gradually along a broad ridge, keeping to its right edge.

Bear right around a large rock outcrop and reach a utility pole.

As the ridge narrows, turn left down into a gully.

Cross the stream bed and bear left up the opposite side of the gully.

Contour around the foot of a side ridge through large guava trees.

Work right, up a partially open ridge.

Bear left off the ridge line into a broad gully.

Cross a very small stream bed and reach a junction (map point B). Take the right fork up the side of the gully. (The trail to the left is the return leg of the Wai'anae Kai loop.)

Gain the ridge line and climb steeply.

The trail switchbacks twice and then resumes going straight up.

Enter the native forest with uluhe ferns and large koa trees.

Keep to the right edge of the ridge.

Then, work left across the ridge face to the other side.

Reach the top of Kamaile'unu Ridge and a trail junction (map point C). Turn right up the ridge. (The trail down the ridge to the left is the return leg of the Wai'anae Kai loop.)

Almost immediately reach an overlook of Wai'anae Valley by some metal utility poles (elev. 2,720 ft).

Continue up the ridge through a flat, forested area.

Break out into the open and climb steadily through grass and native vegetation.

The ridge broadens and levels through an Australian tea grove.

Negotiate a series of large boulders on a steep and narrow section of the ridge. The last boulder is the worst. Initially, skirt it to the right and then work back to the left. There is a cable for assistance.

Climb very steeply through native forest on a broad ridge. There are four cables on this section.

Cut across the face of the ridge to the right and then resume steep climbing. There are another three cables for assistance.

The angle of ascent decreases as the top nears.

Enter the Ka'ala Natural Area Reserve, marked by a sign.

Reach the Ka'ala plateau and bog (map point D).

Cross the bog on a narrow boardwalk.

Reach a low fence and go through the unlocked gate.

Cross a flat, grassy helipad.

Reach the paved Mt. Ka'ala Rd. and the summit (elev. 4,025 ft) (map point E) near the main gate of an FAA radar installation.

For a view of the north shore turn left down the road. Just past a yellow concrete culvert on the right, turn right on a grassy road. Pass a small tower on the right and reach the view point (map point F).

Notes

The Wai'anae Ka'ala hike climbs to O'ahu's highest peak from the leeward side. The route starts in a hot, dry valley and ends in a cool, wet bog with an incredibly rich variety of native Hawaiian plants. The misty walk through the bog is one of the great hiking experiences on the island. After that, the summit, with its road and radars, is an anticlimax.

From the view point on the top you can see all of the north shore and the towns of Waialua and Hale'iwa. The Wahiawā plain and the Ko'olau Range are in the distance to the right. On the way up are views of Wai'anae and Lualualei valleys on the right and Mākaha Valley on the left.

The sections through the boulders and just below the top are extremely narrow and slippery. Watch your balance and footing constantly. Test all cables before using them. If the weather is bad or you just don't feel up to it, turn around.

While crossing the bog, stay on the boardwalk to avoid damaging the vegetation. Don't enter the FAA radar installation even though the main gate is sometimes open. They don't welcome tourists!

The trails making up this hike receive periodic maintenance. The lower and middle sections overgrow slowly between clearings and so are usually open. The steep section just below the top of Mt. Ka'ala has been taken over by blackberry bushes. Wear gloves and long pants for protection against the thorns.

The Mt. Ka'ala Rd. leads down to Farrington Hwy on the Mokulē'ia side. The road is not a good exit because it is long, boring, hard on the feet and knees, and closed to the public. For a superb traverse of the mountain, combine the Wai'anae Ka'ala and Dupont hikes.

The climb up to the utility pole overlook is also part of the Wai'anae Kai hike.

51 'Ōhikilolo

Type:	Ungraded ridge
Length:	7 mi round trip
Elev. Gain:	3,000 ft
Danger:	High
Suitable for:	Expert
Location:	Leeward Wai'anae Range before Mākua Valley
Topo Map:	Ka'ena
Access:	Conditional; open to individuals and organized groups with written permission. Contact the Directorate of Facilities Engineering, U.S. Army Support Command, Fort Shafter, HI 96858.

Trailhead Directions

At Punchbowl St. get on the Lunalilo Fwy (H-1) heading 'ewa (west).

Near Middle St. keep left on Rte 78 west (exit 19B, Moanalua Rd.) to 'Aiea.

By Aloha Stadium bear right to rejoin H-1 to Pearl City and on toward Wai'anae.

As the freeway ends near Campbell Industrial Park, continue along the leeward coast on Farrington Hwy (Rte 93).

Pass the Kahe Point power plant on the right.

Drive through Nānākuli, Mā'ili, and Wai'anae town.

The road narrows to two lanes.

Drive through Mākaha and pass Kea'au Beach Park on the left.

Pass 'Ōhikilolo Mākua Ranch on the right.

Pass Kāneana Cave at the foot of the ridge on the right.

Look for a power line crossing the highway. The line has an orange ball strung on it.

Just past the ball is a large turnout on the left with a paved road angling toward the beach.

Park in the turnout area next to the highway (map point A).

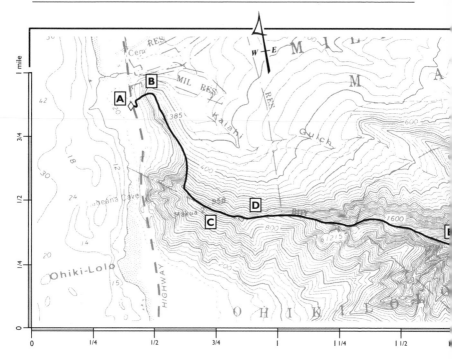

Route Description

Walk back along the left side of Farrington Hwy toward Mākaha. Note the chain-link fence up and on the left.

Pass a utility pole on the left.

Halfway to the next pole turn left and climb the road embankment.

Turn left again paralleling the highway through grass.

Pass the first utility pole.

Reach the fence where it makes a 90-degree turn toward the ridge.

Turn right along the fence.

As it ends, angle left up the slope.

Reach the top of the ridge (map point B) and turn right.

Climb steadily along the crest of the ridge.

Pass an old observation bunker.

Bear right around a rock outcropping.

Descend a small saddle.

Climb steeply, following the right side of the ridge.

As the ridge juts out toward the ocean, switchback right to follow its edge.

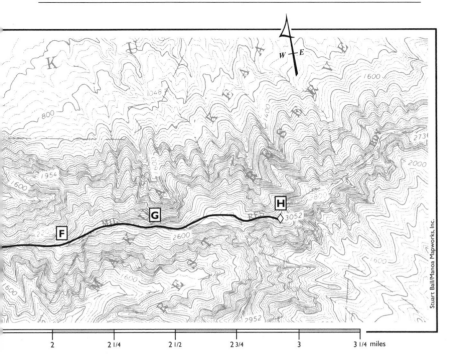

Traverse a series of three humps. On the second are the remains of the Makua 2 triangulation station (map point C).

Descend steeply to a broad saddle (map point D).

Climb, gradually at first, and then more steeply through a rocky section.

Negotiate a narrow rock dike.

Reach the top of a peak marked by two rock outcrops and a silk oak.

Ascend gradually on the narrow ridge.

Pass a second triangulation station and then the Lolo benchmark on the right (map point E).

Reach a second peak with scattered silk oaks at the top and a large side ridge on the right (map point F).

Climb gradually on the open, less-rocky ridge.

Reach a third peak marked by a tape cross on the ground.

Ascend the fourth and fifth peaks, both eroded at the top.

Cross a level bare section.

Enter a forest, first of Christmas berry and then of native plants (map point G).

Skirt a large eroded section on the right.

As the ridge broadens, keep to the right.

Descend briefly and then climb steeply to the top of a triangular peak (elev. 3,052 ft) (map point H). A steep drop-off blocks further progress along the ridge.

Notes

'Ōhikilolo roughly translates as scooped-out brains. Those attempting the hike should perhaps have their heads examined for loss of gray matter!

Seriously, 'Ōhikilolo is the most difficult hike in this book. The climb is steep, the trail is rough and hot, and the danger is considerable. Wear sturdy hiking boots and bring plenty of water.

Views are what this hike is all about. Going up, Mākua Valley is on the left. On the right is 'Ōhikilolo Valley at first and then Mākaha Valley. From the triangular peak you can see Mt. Ka'ala and the rest of the Wai'anae Range. On the left is the north shore and in back is most of the Wai'anae Coast.

On the way down look for the First Hawaiian Bank rec center pool on the left far below. Doesn't it look inviting? Don't you wish you were down there?

If you are interested in native plants, spend some time in the isolated patch of endemic forest near the triangular peak. The forest also has rare native tree snails.

Do 'Ōhikilolo from December through March when the weather is cooler. Keep in mind, however, that a winter storm can make the hike very cold indeed.

Mākua Valley is a military range used for live fire exercises. Do not attempt 'Ōhikilolo when the helicopters are shooting up the valley. Do not descend into the valley because of the unexploded ordnance there.

52 Wai'anae Kai

Type:	Foothill
Length:	3 mi loop
Elev. Gain:	1,300 ft
Danger:	Low
Suitable for:	Intermediate
Location:	Leeward Wai'anae Range above Wai'anae town
Topo Map:	Wai'anae, Ka'ena
Access:	Open

Trailhead Directions

At Punchbowl St. get on the Lunalilo Fwy (H-1) heading 'ewa (west).

Near Middle St. keep left on Rte 78 west (exit 19B, Moanalua Rd.) to 'Aiea.

By Aloha Stadium bear right to rejoin H-1 to Pearl City and on toward Wai'anae.

As the freeway ends near Campbell Industrial Park, continue along the leeward coast on Farrington Hwy (Rte 93).

Drive through Nānākuli and Mā'ili to Wai'anae town.

After passing Burger King on the right, begin counting traffic lights. At the third one, by Wai'anae Coast Drive-In, turn right on Wai'anae Valley Rd.

Reach a bus turnaround marked with white curbs.

Take the one-lane paved road to the left at the back of the circle.

The pavement disappears briefly by some houses and then resumes.

Keep left on the paved road at two junctions. The last one is marked with a large Wai'anae Kai Forest Reserve sign.

Climb steadily through open country.

Pass a water tank on the left.

In a forested area the road levels off momentarily and passes between two concrete buildings surrounded by chain-link fences.

Ascend steeply through the forest.

Reach two concrete buildings and the end of the paved road.

Park on the right off the road near the buildings (map point A).

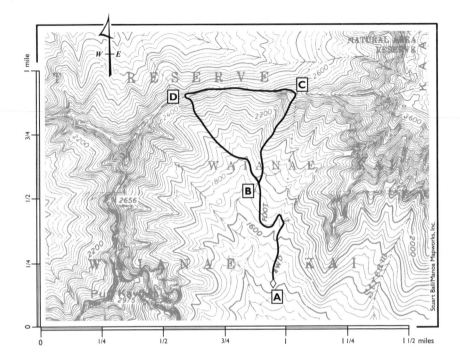

Route Description

Continue up the road (now dirt) to its end at a turnaround loop.

On the right of the loop take the trail marked by four boulders.

Ascend gradually along a broad ridge, keeping to its right edge.

Bear right around a large rock outcrop and reach a utility pole.

As the ridge narrows, turn left down into a gully.

Cross the stream bed and bear left up the opposite side of the gully.

Contour around the foot of a side ridge through large guava trees.

Work right, up a partially open ridge.

Bear left off the ridge line into a broad gully.

Cross a very small stream bed and reach a junction (map point B). Take the right fork up the side of the gully. (The trail to the left is the return leg of the loop.)

Gain the ridge line and climb steeply.

The trail switchbacks twice and then resumes going straight up.

Enter the native forest with uluhe ferns and large koa trees.

Keep to the right edge of the ridge.

Then, work left across the ridge face to the other side.

Reach the top of Kamaile'unu Ridge (map point C) and turn right up it.

Reach an overlook of Wai'anae Valley by some metal utility poles (elev. 2,720 ft).

Backtrack down the ridge and keep right on it. (The trail to the left was the route up.)

Descend, steeply at first, and then more gradually to the low point of a saddle in the ridge.

As the trail begins to climb, reach a junction in a small clearing. Stay on the ridge. (To the left a trail leads down into Wai'anae Valley.)

Reach a second junction in a larger clearing (map point D). Turn left down into Wai'anae Valley. (The ridge trail continues straight.) To the right is a good view of Mākaha Valley.

Descend steeply along a side ridge.

Halfway down, a contour trail comes in on the left. Continue straight down.

Reach the end of the side ridge where two stream beds converge in a gully.

Almost immediately climb out of the gully to the left.

Contour around another side ridge.

Reach the junction with the route going up (map point B). Turn right and retrace your steps back to the car (map point A).

Notes

Wai'anae Kai is all ups and downs. It wanders around the back of Wai'anae Valley in the shadow of Mt. Ka'ala, O'ahu's tallest peak. On the route are some good examples of native plants requiring a drier climate.

From the utility pole overlook you can see Wai'anae Valley all the way to the ocean. To the rear is Mākaha Valley. To the left loom the indented flanks of Mt. Ka'ala (elev. 4,025 ft).

This hike is rated intermediate because of the steep ascents and descents on rough, unimproved trails. In addition, the trails are sometimes ill-defined, and the junctions, sometimes obscure. Follow the description closely.

You can take a side trip to an unnamed peak (elev. 3,000 ft) on Kamaile'unu Ridge. Instead of turning down into Wai'anae Valley right away, continue straight on the ridge trail. There are some great views but be careful in the narrow spots.

The trails making up this hike receive periodic maintenance. They overgrow slowly between clearings and so are usually open.

The climb up to the utility pole overlook is also part of the Wai'anae Ka'ala hike.

53 Kuaokalā

Type:	Foothill
Length:	6 mi loop
Elev. Gain:	800 ft
Danger:	Low
Suitable for:	Novice, Intermediate
Location:	Leeward Wai'anae Range above Ka'ena Point
Topo Map:	Ka'ena
Access:	Conditional; open to individuals and organized groups with a permit. Obtain one from the Forestry and Wildlife Division, Department of Land and Natural Resources, Room 325, 1151 Punchbowl St. (phone 587–0166).

Trailhead Directions

At Punchbowl St. get on the Lunalilo Fwy (H-1) heading 'ewa (west).

Near Middle St. keep left on Rte 78 west (exit 19B, Moanalua Rd.) to 'Aiea.

By Aloha Stadium bear right to rejoin H-1 to Pearl City and on toward Wai'anae.

As the freeway ends near Campbell Industrial Park, continue along the leeward coast on Farrington Hwy (Rte 93).

Pass the Kahe Point power plant on the right.

Drive through Nānākuli, Mā'ili, and Wai'anae town.

The road narrows to two lanes.

Drive through Mākaha and pass Kea'au Beach Park on the left.

On the right pass 'Ōhikilolo Mākua Ranch and then Mākua Military Reservation with its observation post.

Reach the end of the paved highway at Keawa'ula (Yokohama) Bay.

Turn right on the access road to the Ka'ena Point Satellite Tracking Station.

Show your permit to the guard at the station and get a visitor pass.

Switchback up Kuaokalā Ridge.

At its top turn right at the T intersection on Road B.

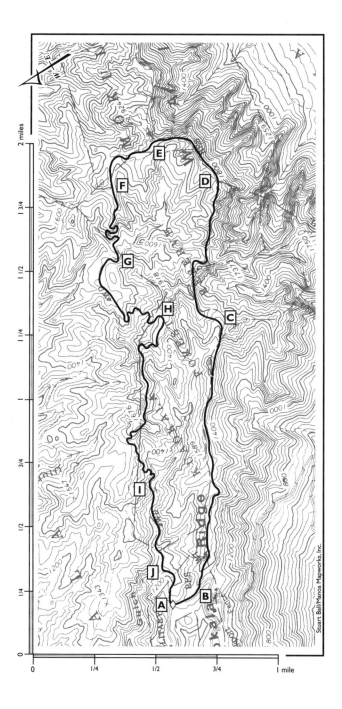

Stuart Ball/Manoa Mapworks, Inc.

Curve left by the main administration building.

Pass a paved one-lane road coming in on the right through some ironwood trees.

After a short descent look for a dirt lot on the right. It's just after another paved one-lane road comes in on the right.

Park in the lot (map point A).

Route Description

Walk back up the main paved road.

By a grove of ironwood trees turn left and up on the one-lane paved road (map point B).

At its end bear right around the fence enclosing a water tank.

Follow the ridge through ironwoods and introduced pines.

Contour on the right side of the ridge below its top.

Descend briefly into a shallow, wooded ravine. Climb alongside it.

At the end of the ravine turn left along the edge of the ridge (map point C).

After crossing an eroded area, contour below the ridge line.

Traverse a narrow bare section.

Climb briefly to a copse of ironwood trees.

Pass puka (hole) rock on the right.

Ascend a small hill to an overlook of Mākua Valley (map point D).

Bear left along the rim of the valley.

Cross an open grassy stretch.

Pass another overlook with rock slabs.

Descend briefly and then climb steeply to reach a junction (elev. 1,960 ft) (map point E). Turn left, away from the rim, on a dirt road. (The trail to the right leads to the Mokulēʻia firebreak road and the Mākua Rim Trail.)

Reach a four-way junction. Continue straight across and downhill on the well-traveled Mokulēʻia firebreak road.

Reach a junction with the Keālia Trail (map point F). Keep left and down on the main road. (To the right, the Keālia Trail, which is actually a road, leads down to Dillingham Air Field on the Mokulēʻia side.)

As the road splits, bear left downhill into Keʻekeʻe Gulch.

Cross a stream (map point G) and ascend gradually out of the gulch.

Switchback steeply to the top of a ridge (map point H).

Descend and then bear left as the road forks.

At the next fork keep right.

The road forks again by some gateposts. Bear left and down.

Descend into Manini Gulch (map point I) and parallel the stream bed.

Reach the end of a paved road by a water pump (map point J).

Take the road up out of the gulch.

Reach the dirt parking lot on the right (map point A).

Notes

If you're tired of doing the same old trails around Honolulu, try this hike for a change of pace. It loops around the cliffs, ridges, and gulches in back of Ka'ena Point. Instead of lush forest, you will see the muted browns and greens of the leeward Wai'anae foothills. It's a far cry from the Makiki-Tantalus hike.

Outbound, there are spectacular views of the leeward coast and Mākua Valley. On the way back the north shore comes into view. Watch for the fixed-wing gliders soaring above Dillingham Air Field.

The best time to do this hike is February through April. The weather is cooler then, and you'll avoid the pig- and bird-hunting seasons.

Do not descend into Mākua Valley. It is a military range used for live fire exercises.

The trail on this hike receives regular maintenance. It overgrows slowly between clearings and so is usually open. Some parts of the trail are graded, and the footing is usually solid. The bare sections, however, can be slippery when wet.

Recently completed is a new trail which bypasses the initial road walk to the water tank. The trail starts near the parking lot by a Smokey the Bear sign.

The initial road section on the way back is also part of the Keālia hike.

The Mokulē'ia firebreak road follows the crest of the Wai'anae Range toward an abandoned Nike missile site. Before reaching it, the road contours around the site and connects with its paved access road. The Mākua Rim Trail starts in back of the Nike site and follows the edge of Mākua Valley.

Kuaokalā provides the best access for one of O'ahu's few good camping trips. It's a 2- or 3-day trip to the Mokulē'ia campsite. Take the outbound leg of the Kuaokalā hike and turn right on the firebreak road. Follow it to its end and turn left down the paved Nike site access road. Turn right on the dirt road heading up through Peacock Flats. The road becomes a trail that ends at a campsite near the Pahole Natural Area Reserve and the Mākua Rim Trail. If you have a layover day, explore along the rim trail toward Mt. Ka'ala. On the last day take the Mākua Rim Trail back to the Nike site. Turn left and descend to the firebreak road. Turn left again to get back to the satellite tracking station.

APPENDIX: CLOSED HIKES

Listed below with a short description are hikes that are not open to the general public. They are classified as CLOSED for one of several reasons.
1. The landowner will not grant permission under any circumstance.
2. The landowner may grant permission but with such onerous conditions attached as to make the hike impractical to do.
3. Getting the necessary permissions is too complicated and time consuming for the average individual. The two clubs mentioned in the introduction can sometimes get permission to do hikes in this third category. Check their schedules.

In any case, if you attempt to do CLOSED hikes on your own, you are trespassing.

Castle
Castle is the finest hike on the island. The trail climbs the steep west wall of Punalu'u Valley by a series of spectacular switchbacks. The route then crosses Kaluanui Stream well above Sacred Falls and continues to the top of the Ko'olau Range and the junction with the Ko'olau Summit Trail.

Ha'ikū Stairs
The Ha'ikū Stairs is a metal stairway that ascends the windward Ko'olau cliffs in back of Kāne'ohe. The stairs start from the U.S. Coast Guard Omega Station in Ha'ikū Valley and top out near the summit of Pu'u Keahi a Kahoe. The climb is near vertical in spots.

Hālawa Ridge
Hālawa Ridge is another long graded hike in the leeward Ko'olau Range. The route starts in North Hālawa Valley and then ascends steeply to the ridge separating the north and south valleys. The trail follows that ridge all the way to the Ko'olau summit.

Hidden Valley
The Hidden Valley hike climbs the precipitous cliffs in back of Swanzy Beach Park in Ka'a'awa. The trail ends at the top of a waterfall in a small lush valley.

Ka'au Crater

Ka'au is a little-known crater nestled against the Ko'olau summit. The hike initially follows Wai'ōma'o Stream in Pālolo Valley. A difficult climb past three waterfalls leads to the rim of the crater and to the top of the Ko'olau Range.

Kaipapa'u

Kaipapa'u is a short hike near Hau'ula. The route follows Kaipapa'u Stream and then climbs the ridge on the right.

Ka'iwa Ridge

Ka'iwa Ridge is a windy hike in the hills above Lanikai.

Kaluanui Ridge

Kaluanui Ridge is the easiest hike to the Ko'olau summit. The route starts in back of the Mariner's Ridge subdivision in Hawai'i Kai.

Kamaile'unu

Kamaile'unu is the most rugged hike on the island. The trail climbs partway up the ridge separating Wai'anae and Mākaha valleys.

Kapālama

Kapālama is a beautiful loop hike in the Ko'olau foothills above the Kamehameha Schools and the O'ahu Country Club.

Kīpapa Ridge

Kīpapa Ridge is the longest, wildest hike on O'ahu. The route starts near Mililani and climbs the ridge south of Kīpapa Stream. The hike ends at the top of the Ko'olau Range near the junction with the start (end) of the Ko'olau Summit Trail.

Kōnāhuanui

Kōnāhuanui is the name given to the twin summits above Nu'uanu Pali. At 3,150 ft the taller of the two is the highest peak in the Ko'olau Range. The route starts at the Nu'uanu Valley overlook and climbs steeply, first to the shorter and then to the taller peak.

Kuolani-Waianu

Kuolani-Waianu is an intricate loop hike that wanders around the back of Waiāhole Valley. The route crosses two major streams, Waianu and Uwao.

Māʻeliʻeli (Puʻu)
Puʻu Māʻeliʻeli is the small peak overlooking Kāneʻohe Bay between Kahaluʻu and Kāneʻohe. The climb to its top is short, but steep.

Makapuʻu-Tom-Tom
Makapuʻu-Tom-Tom offers summit hiking at its best. The route along the cliffs starts near Makapuʻu lookout and ends in Waimānalo. The descent is via the Tom-Tom Trail.

Mauna ʻŌahi
Mauna ʻŌahi is a fascinating valley-ridge combination in back of Hawaiʻi Kai. The valley is Kaʻalākei, and the ridge is Mauna ʻŌahi. The hike has a short section along the Koʻolau summit.

Maunawili
Maunawili is a short, muddy hike to a large, deep swimming hole in Maunawili Stream. The route starts in back of the Maunawili subdivision.

Mokulēʻia
Mokulēʻia is a pleasant hike to the top of the Waiʻanae Range. The route starts in pasture land near Mokulēʻia and ends at an overlook of Mākua Valley.

ʻŌhulehule (Puʻu)
Puʻu ʻŌhulehule is the craggy peak that dominates the windward coast from Kahaluʻu to Punaluʻu. The climb to its summit along the southeast ridge is the most dangerous hike on the island.

Olympus (Mt.)
Mt. Olympus is the massive peak on the Koʻolau summit between Mānoa and Pālolo valleys. The route starts on Waʻahila Ridge at the Kolowalu junction and ascends gradually to the top.

Ulupaina
Ulupaina is a short loop hike in the Koʻolau foothills above Kāneʻohe.

Waiʻalae Nui
Waiʻalae Nui is a superb ungraded ridge hike. The trail starts in back of the Waiʻalae Nui subdivision and climbs to the Koʻolau summit.

Waiau

Waiau is a tough ungraded ridge hike to the Koʻolau summit. The last ½ mile is still under construction. The route starts above Newtown Estates.

Waikāne

Waikāne is two hikes in one. The first is a pleasant stroll through Waikāne Valley. The second is a breathtaking climb to the top of the Koʻolau Range and the junction with the Koʻolau Summit Trail.

Waimalu Ditch

Waimalu Ditch is a valley hike with some great swimming holes. The trail starts above Pearlridge and follows Waimalu Stream.

Wiliwilinui

Wiliwilinui is one of the easiest hikes to the Koʻolau summit because much of it is along a dirt road. The route starts above the Waiʻalae Iki 5 subdivision and proceeds up Wiliwilinui Ridge.

REFERENCES

Bier, James A. Map of Oʻahu, 4th ed. Honolulu: University of Hawaii Press, 1992.

Bier, James A. Oʻahu Reference Maps, 3d ed. Champaign, Ill.

Bryan's Sectional Maps of Oʻahu, 1991 ed. Honolulu: EMIC Graphics, 1990.

Department of Health, Epidemiology Branch. Leptospirosis in Hawaii (pamphlet). Honolulu, 1987.

Department of Land and Natural Resources. Island of Oahu Recreation Map. Honolulu, 1979.

Department of Land and Natural Resources. State Forest Hiking Trails, Island of Oahu (map). Honolulu.

Department of Land and Natural Resources. Trails, Hunting and Park Areas, Island of Oahu (map). Honolulu.

Hawaii Audubon Society. *Hawaii's Birds*. Honolulu, 1989.

Merlin, Mark David. *Hawaiian Forest Plants*. Honolulu: Oriental Publishing Company, 1980.

Pukui, Mary Kawena, and Samuel H. Elbert. *Hawaiian Dictionary*. Honolulu: University of Hawaii Press, 1986.

Pukui, Mary Kawena, Samuel H. Elbert, and Esther T. Mookini. *Place Names of Hawaii*. Honolulu: University of Hawaii Press, 1981.

Sohmer, S. H., and R. Gustafson. *Plants and Flowers of Hawaiʻi*. Honolulu: University of Hawaii Press, 1987.

INDEX

About the Author

Stuart M. Ball, Jr., has been hiking the trails of O'ahu for two decades. Much of that time he has been a hike leader for the Hawaiian Trail and Mountain Club, and he served as president of the club.

He holds a BA from Dartmouth College and an MBA from Stanford University. He is Cost/Profitability Manager at the Bank of Hawaii in Honolulu.

 Production Notes

Composition and paging were done on the
Quadex Composing System and typesetting
on the Compugraphic 8400 by the design
and production staff of University of
Hawaii Press.

The text and display typeface is Gill Sans.

Offset presswork and binding were done by
Malloy Lithographing, Inc. Text paper is
Glatfelter Offset Vellum, basis 50.